Union with Christ

James A. Fowler

C.I.Y. PUBLISHING
P.O. BOX 1822
FALLBROOK, CALIFORNIA 92088-1822

www.christinyou.net

Union with Christ

Christ *in* us,
Christ *as* us,
Christ *through* us

Published by:
C.I.Y. PUBLISHING
P.O. BOX 1822
FALLBROOK, CALIFORNIA 92088-1822

ISBN 978-1-929541-03-4

Scriptural quotations are from the New American Standard Bible, copyrights 1960, 1962, 1963, 1968,1972, 1973, 1975 by the Lockman Foundation, LaHabra, California.

Printed in the United States of America

Acknowledgements

Our thoughts inevitably have connections with what others have thought, spoken, and written. Acknowledgement of some of those persons who have been instrumental in the formation of the ideas presented in this book is in order.

My first introduction to the concept of "union with Christ" was through the teaching and writing of Norman P. Grubb. Though his teachings have often been taken to the extreme, the central thesis of "union with Christ" is biblically documented and theologically orthodox. The first section of this book is an attempt to verify the legitimacy of the concept of "union with Christ," while at the same time providing cautionary arguments to avoid the extremisms of pantheism and monism. I am grateful to the planners of the Northern Virginia Bible Group Conference in New Windsor, Maryland in October 2002 for providing the platform where this thesis was first presented.

The writing of *Christ in us, as us, and through us* actually preceded the development and writing of *Union with Christ*, and was first published as a small booklet.

For facilitating the editing and formatting of this present volume, I express my gratitude to my sister, Sylvia Burnett, without whose impetus and assistance this book would likely never have materialized.

My wonderful wife, Gracie, always deserves acknowledgment for her consistent encouragement of every facet of my involvement in Christian ministry.

To God be the glory!

James A. Fowler (2005)

UNION WITH CHRIST: Seeking a Balanced Understanding
Copyright ©2003 by James A. Fowler.

Contents

Introduction

Did you ever play the children's game where one person whispers a phrase to another, and that person to another, and the whispering action continues down the line or around the circle? What the last person hears (or thinks he hears) seldom resembles the statement that was originally made.

The Christian expressions concerning "union with Christ" have been muddled in a similar manner, and are complicated even more by the fact that the original biblical statements about the Christian life did not refer directly or explicitly to the phrase, "union with Christ." It was centuries after Christ's historical incarnation that Latin Christian writers began to refer to *unio cum Christo*, "union with Christ."

As that phrase was passed down the line in Christian circles through the subsequent centuries of Christian thought, it became very convoluted with many accretions of doctrinal and devotional understanding. This study will seek to discover a biblically balanced understanding of the Christian's "union with Christ."

It will be instructive to commence with a brief mention of the definition of "union." "Union" is to be differentiated from "unity." A "unity" is something that exists as one. A "union" is the bringing together, or uniting, of multiple (two or more) distinct, disparate or separate entities, not previously conjoined, but now brought together, joined, formed, unified, and united into a singular entity.

Using this distinction of definition, it would not be proper to speak of *Trinitarian union*, for the divine Trinity is a tri-unity wherein the Father, Son and Holy Spirit have existed in eternal unity and oneness. Despite the contention of Arius that "there was a time when the Son was not," the orthodox Christian understanding denies that there was a time when particular persons of the Godhead did not exist or were brought into being, and subsequently a time or occasion when the separate persons of the Godhead were conjoined in a "union."

———————— ✳ ————————

The Trinity of God has always existed as a tri-unity of divine oneness.[1]

At the heart of Christian teaching, however, is the unique and singular historical act of the Son of

God being united with humanity in the "union" of the God-man. This *Christological union* was the union of deity and humanity in a particular historical individual, Jesus Christ. The functional objective of the *Christological union* is also expressed as the *mediatorial union*, for Jesus Christ as the God-man was "the one mediator between God and man" (I Tim. 2:5).

The particular means of the uniting of God and man in the historical person of Jesus Christ is referred to as the *incarnational union*. The apostle John explained that the divine *Logos*, the eternal Son of God Who "was God" (John 1:1), was incarnated in physical flesh as a man. "The Word became flesh" (John 1:14). This *incarnational union* was a singularly unique union. There was only one Son of God, the divine Word (*Logos*), and the historical singularity of His being incarnated as a man was "once and for all."

The reason this emphasis is necessary is due to the common usage of *incarnational union* among some Christians in reference to the union of the Christian with Christ. If the phrase *incarnational union* is to be used to explain the Christian's subjective union with Christ, adequate clarification must continually be made between the singular historical event of the Son of God becoming a man when "the Word became flesh" (John 1:14) and the generalized or generic use of the word "incarnational" to refer to the embodiment or enfleshment of the life of Jesus in the Christian.

Christian theology has traditionally explained the *Christological union* of *incarnational union* as the *hypostatic union* of deity and humanity in the Person of Jesus. Since the Council of Chalcedon in A.D. 451, Christian theology has sought to explain that the two natures, or substances, or essences, or essential properties of deity and humanity were united in the union of a distinct individual or person (Greek *hypostasis*), i.e., Jesus.

Again, we must point out that this was a singularly unique *hypostatic union*, an unrepeatable singularity of divine action, because some have attempted to use *hypostatic union* to explain a substantial, essential union of two natures (deity and humanity) in the Christian when the Christian is united with Christ.

Chapter *1*

Historical and Theological Review

When we begin to consider the Christian's "union with Christ," which is contingent upon the historic foundation of the *Christological union* of the Person of Jesus Christ, we find a quagmire of semantic and interpretive confusion throughout the literature of Christian history. What we discover is that the term "union" has been employed in a multitude of different ways.

The first major differentiation in explaining "union with Christ" is between the attempts to explain "union with Christ" in terms of an *objective union*, a union effected outside of and external to the person and experience of the individual Christian, and those explanations of "union with Christ" as a *subjective union* that takes place internally within the person and experience of the Christian individual.

Objective Union

Concepts of *objective union* with Christ sometimes begin with the *race union* of Christ with mankind. As the Son of Man, Jesus was united with humanity as the federal head of the human race. This *race union* is explained as a *federal union* or a *judicial union* or a *legal union* of Christ's *representative union* or *solidarity union* with mankind.

In the predestined plan of God, and by the predetermined decrees of God, it is alleged that those who were predestined, elected, and called of God are united with Christ in *election union*; and that, often in the context of a *covenantal union* of God's people. This *objective union* of Christ's *identification union* or *vicarious union* with mankind is often referred to as the *vital union* of Christ with man in an objectified *positional union*.

Both Roman Catholic and Protestant theologians proceed to explain the *objective union* of Christians with Christ in the *collective union* or *corporation union* that all Christians have with Christ in the body of Christ, the church. This *ecclesial union, ecclesiastical union,* or *church union* is usually closely aligned with the *sacramental union* that Christians are said to have with Christ as the church administers the sacraments that are alleged to establish *baptismal union* and *eucharistic union* with Christ.

The *collective church union* that Christians have with Christ in the body of Christ is often called an *organic union* with Christ, based on the fact that the church is not just an institution or organization, but an organism, a body united to Christ as head (Eph. 1:22,23; Col. 1:18; Rom. 12:15; I Cor. 12:27).

The *historic co-active union* with Christ is often explained by the *crucifixion union, resurrection union,* and *ascension union* of the Christian's being united with Christ in co-crucifixion (cf. Gal. 2:20; Rom. 6:5,6; Col. 2:12; 3:1) and identification with the historical acts of Jesus Christ. This is also referred to as the *positional union* of *identification union* with Christ. The Christian has been united "in Christ," so that when He died we died, when He was raised we were raised, and when He ascended we ascended in *historic co-active union* with Christ.

Theological concepts of *objective union* with Christ also include the expected *eschatological union* with Christ in the *final-state union* or *heavenly union*—the *consummation union* of the *eternal union* of *glory union* when Christians hope to be involved in *reigning union* with Christ.

The theologians sum up all of the above-mentioned concepts of *objective union* with Christ as *mystical union,* for they are regarded as the great mysteries of Christian thought and theology.

Subjective Union

Others who want to focus on the *subjective union* of Christ with Christians would prefer to reserve the phrase *mystical union* for the internal "mystery ... which is Christ in you, the hope of glory" (Col. 1:27). If ever there was a phrase that has become "all things to all people," it is this phrase *unio mystica*, or *mystical union*. It is even employed in the kabbalist teachings of Judaism, as well as in Islamic and Buddhist teaching. Its extensive usage has rendered it a rather inane and meaningless phrase for the discussion of "union with Christ."

The Christian's *subjective union* with Christ is often identified as a *spiritual union* based on the Pauline statement that "the one who joins himself to the Lord is one spirit (with Him)" (I Cor. 6:17).

---------- ✳ ----------

When an individual is "born of the Spirit" (John 3:5,6), a *spiritual union* of the Spirit of Christ and the spirit of that person is established (Rom. 8:9,16).

This has been called *regenerative union, saving union*, or *new-creation union*, although distinction in these terms can and should be made.

Evangelical theology has often referred to the *faith union* effected between Christ and the Christian when the supplied life of God's grace in Christ is received in the derivation of faith-receptivity. In this *fiduciary union* a *personal union* is established. It is a *relational union* that is likened to the *conjugal union* of *marital union* (Eph. 5:28-30) between husband and wife. This *personal union* of the Christian with Christ is more than a union of alliance or mere personal relationship, for it involves the deepest intimacy of oneness in *spiritual union* and *relational union*.

Spiritual life union with Christ is to be expressed in the *practical union* of Christian living. This functional and *operational union* with the dynamic life of Christ has been termed *experimental union, experiential union,* and *existential union.*

In many cases this has been regarded as a *progressive union* of behavioral ideals that are to be attained or achieved through various spiritual disciplines of meditation, prayer, Bible reading, liturgical exercises, dying to self, etc. Such religious "works" are regarded as developmental for attaining *confessional union, obedience union, transformational union,* and myriad forms of *moral union* with Christ by confessing, obeying, and keeping His commands.

A more biblical perspective realizes that a real *spiritual union* with Christ has been established in *regenerative union* with the indwelling Spirit of Christ. This *new-creature union* (II Cor. 5:17) has created such oneness of spirit between Christ and the

Christian (I Cor. 6:17) that the spirit of man has no capacity or capability to function apart from the Spirit of Christ. The living Lord Jesus within us has become the basis of a *vital union* whereby a Christ-one, a Christian, lives out Christ's life in a *manifestational union* or an *evidentiary union*, which others have called a *life union* or *sanctification union*.

Reference to *incarnational union* (referred to above) and the enfleshment of Christ's life in Christian behavior, finds some biblical justification in Paul's statement of the "life of Jesus manifested in our mortal flesh (or body)" (II Cor. 4:10,11).

As we "abide in Christ" (John 6:56; 15:4-7; I John 2:24) in *abiding union*, such a *fellowship union* allows for union to become communion, even to the extent of *intercessory union* that allows the life of Christ to be laid down and lived out for others through us.

Misleading Union

We must beware, however, of allowing the *subjective union* of *spiritual union* with Christ to be cast as a *metaphorical union* that is nothing more than a figure of speech rather than an actual *spiritual union*. Neither should "union with Christ" be portrayed as merely a *psychological union* that causes one to attempt to think, feel and will in accord with Christ's example, as the separated Spirit seeks to induce such by *influential union*. The objective of union with Christ is not to experience a *consciousness union* that is continually conscious of Jesus, or an *ecstatic union* that gets "high" on sensate emotions.

Caution must also be observed in allowing *spiritual union* with Christ to be formulated into the varying forms of *metaphysical union* that postulate an *essential union* or a *consubstantial union* whereby man becomes substantially fused, merged, or commingled with God in a *deification union.*

References to *hypostatic union* or *organic union* of the Christian individual with Christ lend themselves to concepts of *coalescence union* or *virtual union* that can depersonalize and deify the human individual. This is also present in the monistic and pantheistic emphases of oneness with God that promote a *universalistic union* of all men with God, wherein "God is all in all."

"Union Life"

In this review of how Christian theology has addressed the concept of "union with Christ," we have observed the objective and subjective senses of Christ's union with man through Christian history. But specifically within the subjective interpretations of "union with Christ" where Christ's presence affects us internally, there is a void in the history of Christian teaching, an absence of explanation, of how "union with Christ" affects who we are, our identity.

That particular emphasis of *identity union* was the focus of Norman P. Grubb, and others who followed him.

In the twentieth century there was a movement called "union life." Via the teachings and writings of Norman Grubb, there was an emphasis on the Christian's *spiritual union* with Christ. A periodical magazine entitled "Union Life" was published for many years. It heralded the Christian's *union-identity* with Christ, as did Grubb's last two books, *Who Am I?* and *Yes I Am.*

Regrettably, the "union life" movement fractured and splintered in the latter part of the twentieth century, prior to the death of Norman Grubb, and much to his chagrin and sorrow. Failing to maintain a balance of emphasis on regenerative union identity with Christ, the various splinter groups developed divergent emphases:

(1) one group taught that "union life" is *contained* in all men in monistic universalism.

(2) one fellow taught that "union life" is *ordained* for all in inevitable predetermined fatalism.

(3) one group taught that "union life" is *retained* through identification, repudiation, and suppression of sin in group accountability.

(4) one group taught that "union life" is *attained* experientially through the discipline of "centering prayer."

Somewhere along the chain of whispers, they all heard and expressed a distorted message, failing to understand that "union life" is *obtained* by receiving the Spirit of Christ into one's spirit by faith and continuing to derive all from the One Who *is* Life—Jesus Christ.

Chapter 2

Seeking a Balanced Understanding

This study will attempt to illustrate, in the graphic form of a chart, the necessary balance and tension that must be maintained if we are to have a biblical and theological tenable teaching of "union with Christ."

The format we will employ to seek this balanced understanding will be the context of dialectic. Our first order of business will be to differentiate dialectic from other forms of divided thinking.

A *dichotomy* is a division of elements into two parts. Etymologically the word means, "to cut in two." A dichotomy is a bifurcation of elements, separated and distinguished. The constitution of man is often explained as a dichotomy of body and soul, or alternatively as a trichotomy of body, soul, and spirit. Man, however, is not "cut in two" or "cut in three," but is a functional whole with physical, psychological and spiritual function.

Dualism in its most generic meaning simply refers to two elements or substances. As a classic philosophical concept it refers to two opposing principles or powers, often regarded as being equal and counterbalanced. One power is identified with good, and the other with evil. The *yin-yang* dualism of oriental philosophy is an example where good and evil are equally balanced.

The Platonic dualism of spirit and matter presented a constant conflict of good and evil: spirit being identified with good, and matter with evil. One approach to avoiding the conflict was to give in to the evil of physical matter, and indulge oneself in hedonism and Epicureanism. Another approach was to avoid the evil of the material by denial in asceticism and monasticism. Neither approach solved the dualism.

Sometimes opposites are cast as *antinomies*, meaning "against the law" of reason. When opposing principles or tenets form an unreasonable and irresolvable contradiction, this is an antinomy.

A *paradox* is very similar to an antinomy. It involves opposing truths that do not have an apparent logical solution. They are juxtaposed alongside of each other in order to note their distinction.

Dialectic

Dialectic is a process of thought where a concept is preserved and fulfilled by its opposite. Opposite tenets are held in tensioned balance, creating a logical dialogue of how they relate to each other. This is not necessarily the Socratic method of thesis and antithesis seeking a logical synthesis. Rather, it involves living with the contradictory opposites and finding completeness and totality only in the counterbalance of the two, allowing a dynamic interchange and interplay of two concepts to challenge and balance each other.

The Western mind, steeped as it is in the linear cause and effect of Aristotelian logic, has a difficult time with dialectic. Western thought wants to get everything figured out, systematized, organized, categorized, and boxed up in the absoluteness of an airtight system with no loose ends. The Eastern mind, on the other hand, seems more able to maintain opposites in tension, perhaps because there has often been a dualistic base to their thinking.

By way of personal testimony, I can admit that I was a product of my Western world, even to the extent of being a religious fundamentalist with absolutist thinking of right and wrong, good and evil, orthodoxy and heresy. I came to understand philosophical dialectic through the writings of the Danish author Soren Kierkegaard. Theological dialectic was learned through the writings of the Swiss theologian Karl Barth. The writings of the French sociologist Jacques Ellul provided me with sociological dialectic. In personal and spiritual matters the writings of the British missionary Norman P. Grubb provided a perspective of spiritual

17

dialectic. Together these mentors have taught me to view everything in terms of dialectic—to see the other side of everything, in the Bible, in theology, in sociology, and in spiritual matters.

There is such polarity and one-sidedness in Christian thinking today. Calvinism is set against Arminianism, and they both need to see the dialectic of divine sovereignty balanced with human responsibility. In eschatological matters, preterism is on the far side of futurism, and they both need to see the dialectic of the "already" and the "not yet." Dispensationalism battles against Covenant Theology, and they both need to recognize the dialectic of continuity and discontinuity. Creationism opposes scientism, and they both need to find balance in the dialectic of the supernatural alongside of the natural. The Biblicists and the charismatics need to see the dialectic of objectivity and subjectivity. The polarized extremes can only find common ground in an understanding of dialectic.

Having already noted the dialectic of objective and subjective interpretations of "union with Christ," we shall proceed to consider the dialectic of *union* and *distinction* within the subjective understanding of "union with Christ." This is not to deny or deprecate the objective interpretations of "union with Christ," but our intent is to emphasize the subjective "union with Christ." Within this graphic formatting of subjective union we shall observe the sequence of the **"union of being"** and the **"union of doing**." These can also be referred to as *ontological union* and *operational union*, and can also be seen in the tension of dialectic.

Chapter 3

Union of Being

The subjective union of Christ and the Christian is referred to throughout the New Testament literature, and was expressed by early Latin Christian writers in the phrase, *unio cum Christo*. Others used the phrase *unio mystica* or "mystical union," but (as we have previously indicated) this phrase has been so broadly employed in Christian teaching that it is basically meaningless.

Spiritual Union

The apostle Paul wrote, "The one who is joined to the Lord is one spirit (with Him)" (I Cor. 6:17). This "one spirit" *union* of the Christian with Christ is contextualized by the *distinction* of "the one" being joined to "the Lord."

In the preceding verse, I Corinthians 6:16, which quotes from Genesis 2:24, the oneness of the "one flesh" marital union of husband and wife establishes the basis of contrast with the "one spirit" union of Christ and the Christian. The joining in "one flesh" in marriage and the joining in "one spirit" in Christian relationship are both real *unions*, but the *distinction* is evident in that they are relational unions, neither party being diminished or lost in the union of the two.

Writing to the Romans, Paul makes the *distinction* of the *spirit union*, explaining, "The *Spirit* bears witness with our *spirit* that we are children of God" (Rom. 8:16).

––––––––––– ✳ –––––––––––

> The Spirit of Christ relates to the human spirit by the assuring witness that we have an *identity union* with Christ as "children of God."

This requires, of course, the indwelling presence of the Spirit of Christ, for Paul wrote earlier, "If anyone does not have the Spirit of Christ, he is none of His" (Rom. 8:9), i.e., that person is not a Christian if the Spirit of Christ does not dwell in him.

In his epistle to the Galatians, Paul wrote, "I have been crucified with Christ; it is no longer I who lives, but Christ lives in me…" (Gal. 2:20a). Some have interpreted the words, "it is no longer I who lives," to mean Paul's individuality and personality have been annihilated or absorbed into the Christ

Who lives in him or as him. The latter part of the same verse disallows such, for it states the remaining distinction, "...and the life that I now live in the flesh, I live by faith in the Son of God, Who loved me and gave Himself up for me" (Gal. 2:20b). The *distinctions* between the Christian "I" and the "Son of God...Himself" reveal the relationalism of this *spiritual union* between Christ and the Christian.

In the second epistle of Peter we read, "His divine power has granted to us everything pertaining to life and godliness, through the true knowledge of Him Who called us by His own glory and excellence, and granted to us His precious and magnificent promises..., in order that by them you might become partakers of the divine nature" (II Pet. 1:3,4).

There is a union of the Christian with the "divine nature" of Father, Son, and Holy Spirit, but this does not imply that the Christian implicitly or inherently becomes "divine nature" in any kind of fused merging or coalescence. The Christian can never declare, "I am divine nature." Rather, this verse indicates that we are "*partakers* of the divine nature" of the Godhead, and the Greek word *koinonoi* means that we "take part in, share in, and have commonality with" the divine nature of God. *Distinction* is preserved in the *union* with "divine nature," and this is certainly evident in the preceding part of the sentence in the triple distinction of "Him" and "us."

The epistle to the Hebrews also indicates that Christians are "*partakers* of Christ" (Heb. 3:14) and "*partakers* of the Holy Spirit" (Heb. 6:4). A different

Greek word, *metochoi*, is used in these verses, meaning, "to participate in as recipients" (cf. Heb. 3:1; 12:8). In vital union with the persons of the Godhead, Christians are recipient participants with Father, Son and Holy Spirit, but the word "partakers" implies that *distinction* is maintained.

It is the privilege of the Christian to participate and have fellowship with God in intimate communion (common union). "We are called into fellowship with His Son, Jesus Christ" (I Cor. 1:9), and "our fellowship is with the Father, and with His Son, Jesus Christ" (I John 1:3), as well as "fellowship of the Spirit" (Phil. 2:1). The Greek word in all of these verses is *koinonia*, which indicates a commonality of participant relationalism, but does not allow for essential equivalence.

The most used New Testament phrase for the Christian's union with Christ is the simple phrase, "in Christ," or "in Christ Jesus," or simply "in Him." These prepositional phrases are used several hundred times in the New Testament writings.

————————— ✳ —————————

Whenever we read this "in Christ" phrase,
we can legitimately interpret it as
"in union with Christ."

For example: "By His doing you are *in Christ Jesus* (in union with Christ Jesus), Who became to us wisdom, righteousness, and sanctification and redemption" (I Cor. 1:30). "If any man is *in Christ* (in union with Christ), he is a new creature" (II Cor. 5:17).

We have such a spiritual union with the Triune God that "our life is hid with Christ in God" (Col. 3:3), and "Christ is our life" (Col. 3:4). "*In Him* (in union with Him) we have been made complete" (Col. 2:10). "Every spiritual blessing in heavenly places is ours *in Christ Jesus* (in union with Christ Jesus)" (Eph. 1:3) —"all things belong to you" (I Cor. 2:21,22)— "everything pertaining to life and godliness" (II Pet. 1:3). Our union with Christ is such that "we are seated in the heavenly places *in Christ Jesus* (in union with Christ Jesus)" (Eph. 2:6).

Analogies

There are a number of analogies employed by the New Testament writers to illustrate "union with Christ." Every analogy is such that it simultaneously presents *distinction* within the *union*.

The *vessel/contents* analogy. "We (Christians) have this treasure (Christ) in earthen vessels, that the surpassing greatness of the power may be of God and not from ourselves" (II Cor. 4:7). The Christian is the vessel. Christ is the spiritual content. Though distinct, there is a vital union that allows the dynamic of our action to be the power of God.

The *branch/vine* analogy. "Every branch *in Me* (in union with Me)" (John 15:2) "cannot bear fruit of itself, unless it abides in the vine" (John 15:4). Jesus clearly states, "I am the vine, you are the branches; he who abides *in Me* (in union with Me), and I in him, he bears much fruit, for apart from Me, you can do nothing" (John 15:5). The analogy obviously pictures a union between the vine, Christ, and the branch, a Christian. At the same time there is a distinction between the "Me" and the "he"; it is the Christian's responsibility to "abide" in Christ.

The *house/occupant* analogy. Paul refers to "the earthly tent that is our house" (II Cor. 5:1). The occupant of our physical house is intended to be God, allowing for an indwelling union that allows God to control everything that takes place in our house. Though intimately united, the house and the occupant remain distinct.

The *temple/god* analogy. "Do you not know that you are a temple of God, and that the Spirit of God dwells in you?" (I Cor. 3:16). "Do you not know that your body is a temple of the Holy Spirit Who is in you, …and that you are not your own?" (I Cor. 6:19). This analogy has both individual and collective connotations (cf. II Cor. 6:16). Individually and collectively we are the temple in which God is to dwell and reign.

The *body/head* analogy. This analogy is specifically collective, but maintains the distinction of the individual also. "You are Christ's body, and individually members of it" (I Cor. 12:27). "We are one body in Christ, and individually members one of another" (Rom. 12:5). "God gave Him (Christ) as head over all things to the church, which is His body" (Eph. 1:22,23). "He is the head of the body, the church" (Col. 1:18). Head and body obviously form a living union, but are not to be indistinguishably synthesized.

The *wife/husband* analogy. "As the church is to Christ, so ought wives to be to their husbands. Husbands, love your wives as Christ loved the church..." (Eph. 5:24,25). "This mystery is great: I am speaking in reference to Christ and the church" (Eph. 5:32). The relational union of the marital union between husband and wife is the analogous pattern for the spiritual union between Christ and Christians. The "one flesh" union (Gen. 2:24; I Cor. 6:16; Eph. 5:31) is the physical picture of the "one spirit" union (I Cor. 6:17). Distinction between the relational parties is always recognized in the union.

"Christ in you"

These union analogies all retain *distinction* in the elements being *united*. The vessel is not the contents, and the content is not the vessel. The branch is not the vine, and the vine is not the branch. The house is not the occupant, and the occupant is not the house.

The temple is not the god, and the god is not the temple. The body is not the head, and the head is not the body. The wife is not the husband, and the husband is not the wife. Distinction exists within the union of the two.

Some of these analogies (vessel, house, temple) picture the indwelling of Christ in the Christian. Not only is the Christian "in Christ" (in union with Christ), and this is the predominant New Testament phrase, but there are clear biblical statements that the living Lord Jesus, the Spirit of Christ, dwells "in us" as Christians. "It is no longer I who lives, but *Christ lives in me*" (Gal. 2:20). "This is the mystery... *Christ in you*, the hope of glory" (Col. 1:27). "Do you not recognize this about yourselves, that *Jesus Christ is in you*?" (II Cor. 13:5).

The entire Trinitarian God dwells in the Christian. "God abides in us" (I John 4:12,15,16). "If the Spirit of Him Who raised Jesus from the dead lives in you, He will give life through His Spirit Who indwells you" (Rom. 8:11). "By the Holy Spirit Who dwells in us, guard the treasure which has been entrusted to you" (II Tim. 1:14).

Chapter 4

A Change of Identity

We must remember, however, that "union with Christ" goes beyond the distinction of Father, Son and Holy Spirit located within and indwelling the Christian. The location of God in man must be kept balanced by the emphasis on a real "union of being" with God. By the reception of the living God into our spirit in spiritual regeneration, the Christian, the Christ-one, becomes something/someone that he was not before. There is a change of identity; and that, by an *identity union* with Jesus Christ.

Identity Union

The Christian becomes a "new creature *in Christ* (in union with Christ); ...old things have passed away, and all things have become new (spiritually)" (II Cor. 5:17). The Christian becomes a "new man." The "old man was crucified with Christ" (Rom. 6:6). The "old man was laid aside" (Eph. 4:22; Col. 3:9) when we became a Christian. The Christian "has put on the new man...created in righteousness and holiness" (Eph. 4:24), and "renewed in accord with the image of God" (Col. 3:10). The identity of this "new creature" and "new man" is only *in Christ* (in union with Christ).

The New Testament uses many designations for the new *identity union* of the Christian. The Christian is a "child of God" (Rom. 8:16; John 1:12; I John 3:1,2). The Christian is an adopted "son of God" (Rom. 8:17; Gal. 3:16). Christians are referred to as "saints" (Eph. 1:18; 4:12) or "holy ones."

————————— ✳ —————————

Christians are designated by character traits
that can only be understood as a result of our
"union of being" with Christ,
and are not contingent on our doing.

The Christian is identified as "holy and blameless" (Col. 1:22). The Christian is also called "righteous." "Through the obedience of the One (Christ), the many (Christians) are made righteous" (Rom. 5:19). "We become the righteousness of God *in Christ* (in union with Christ)" (II Cor. 5:21). "Christ Jesus has become to us righteousness" (I Cor. 1:30).

Despite the protestations of the Reformers that Christians are only "declared righteous" in a legal and juridical pronouncement from the divine Judge, the scriptural record indicates that we are "made righteous." In fact, Christians "are perfect" (Phil. 3:15), "perfected" (Heb. 10:14), and regarded as "the spirits of righteous men made perfect" (Heb. 12:23).

Christians need to realize that *in Christ* (in union with Christ) they are acceptable to God. "Christ accepted us to the glory of God" (Rom. 15:7). "There is, therefore, now no condemnation for those who are *in Christ Jesus* (in union with Christ Jesus)" (Rom. 8:1).

The world employs an abundance of self-talk about self-image, self-worth, self-value, self-concept, etc., but the Christian can have an assurance of a secure identity that is far greater that the criteria on which the world relies. The Christian can have a "positive personal concept" of who he is *in Christ* (in union with Christ).

Collectively, in the church of Jesus Christ, we also have a *union-identity*. We are the "people of God" (I Pet. 2:10). We are a "royal priesthood" (I Pet. 2:9) of "kings and priests" (Rev. 1:6). Together we are a covenant community (Heb. 8:10,11), comprising the "body of Christ" (I Cor. 12:13; Rom. 12:15).

It is so important for Christians to be aware that their *union-identity*, individually and collectively, is a result of a real "union with Christ." The Christian life is not a charade of play-acting or role-playing, trying to "live like Jesus" and "love like Jesus." The Christian is so spiritually united with Christ, as a Christ-one deriving being and identity from Christ, that it can be said, "There is no explanation for me apart from Him."

Derivation

We are forced to observe *distinction*, though, in the recognition that the Christian is not any of these things "in and of himself," i.e., intrinsically, inherently, self-existently, or self-generatively. Our union of identity is "in Christ" (in union with Christ). It is a derived identity, derived from our "union with Christ."

We are holy ones because
the Holy One, Jesus Christ, lives in us
(Acts 3:14; 4:27,30).

We are righteous ones because
the Righteous One, Jesus Christ, lives in us
(Acts 3:14; 7:52).

We are perfect ones because
the Perfect One, Jesus Christ, lives in us
(Heb. 7:28).

Distinction must be noted in the Christian's derivation from Christ to *be* who we *are*, and *do* what we *do*. God created us as derivative creatures. As derivative man, we always derive from another, a spirit source beyond ourselves. We are not the quality, the virtue, the character, the identity, the action in ourselves. We are not gods, and never become gods or God. There is always the distinction of the divine Supplier and the human receiver or deriver. The basic human function is derivation, dependency, receptivity, i.e., faith. We are responsible choosers, and faith is a choice to receive from, depend on, and derive from another.

Deriving our life, being, and identity from "union with Christ" does not mean that we are "no longer human," as some have claimed. It does not mean that the Christian is no longer a distinct individual with a particular personality.

———————— ✳ ————————

Though identity is formed in our spirit
by "union with Christ," we retain individuality
within the function of our soul.

—————————————————

There is always a distinct "me" that relates to and derives from "He"; even though there is no explanation for "me" apart from "He."

Chapter 5

Evangelical Detachment

Modern evangelicalism has not placed much emphasis on "being," much less "union of being in Christ." American evangelicalism, in particular, has emphasized pragmatic productivity in precepts, procedures and programs for "doing" God's work. Success in the accomplishment of "doing" has become the basis for significance and identity.

Over-objectification

The *distinction* of Christ and the Christian has been pushed to the extreme of an objectified and separated concept of the Christian's relationship with Christ. The vast majority of those who call themselves "Christians" today are essentially deistic in their understanding of God. They view God as a detached and separated deity. "God is up in heaven, and I am down here on earth." In addition, this disjoined deity is regarded as an offended deity who is angry and judgmental about the sinfulness of man. God is viewed as opposed to and against man.

Jesus is likewise regarded as far removed in His transcendence, seated at the right hand of God the Father. There is very little sense of the immanence or internal presence of Jesus in the Christian, much less any sense of "union with Christ." Jesus is usually considered to be interceding for Christians, acting as the legal advocate who is trying to convince the Father to accept us. Such an outlook severs the essential unity of the Trinity.

This detachment of God and man has been fostered by a theological paradigm that has over-objectified the Person and work of Jesus Christ. Their perspective is that Jesus died vicariously in our place on the cross, and then went to heaven before the Father to convince Him to impute certain benefits to those who would assent to His redemptive efficacy. On the basis of Christ's substitutional work, God is then alleged to be willing to grant a new standing, a new status, a new position to those who identify with Jesus, and He will declare them righteous.

------------ ✳ ------------

Instead of an indwelling presence of the Spirit of Christ allowing for a new spiritual identity, evangelicalism has offered identification with the historical and theological Jesus, and more tangibly with the church organization.

Those who would become Christians are encouraged to walk the aisle, raise their hand, and join the group. They must assent to the veracity of the historical and theological Jesus, go to catechism, agree with the creed, and sign the "statement of faith." Having thus become a "member," they must consent to serve on a committee that promotes what the church is "doing."

This offers no real indwelling *union-identity* with the living Lord Jesus, but only a social association in alliance with Jesus. The new church member's casual "personal relationship" with Jesus is assumed because he now has the "wet passport" of a baptismal certificate. New church members are assured that they have received a static deposit of impersonal "eternal life" which will serve as a "ticket to heaven" for future union and intimacy with God.

Their only sense of identity is that they are identified and denominated as a Methodist, a Presbyterian, an Episcopalian, a Baptist, etc., or polarized as a Calvinist or Arminian, a fundamentalist or a charismatic, a dispensationalist or a covenantist, a liberal or a conservative, mainline or non-denominational. There is no sense of a spiritual *union-identity* with the living Lord, only a sense of identification with a belief-system cause or an institutional entity.

Double-minded Duality

In like manner, instead of an awareness of "union with Christ" as "partakers of the divine nature" (II Pet. 1:4), evangelicalism has fostered the double-minded duality of the Christian having two internal natures that are in conflict. This is illustrated by the hypothetical presence of a "black dog" and a "white dog" dwelling within the Christian, and these are involved in a life and death struggle to determine who will win.

What this produces is a schizophrenic understanding of identity that results in a paranoid uncertainty of whether one is being motivated by "self" or Jesus. "Is this me, or is this Jesus?" The confused Christians can then engage in the "denial" of being able to win the behavioral battle, and resign themselves to antinomian sinfulness. Alternatively, they may conscientiously have doubts about their salvation that are relieved through periodical emotional and ecstatic religious experiences or ritual observances.

When evangelicals do attempt to consider who they are, they usually develop a negative sense of "self" that is self-denigrating and self-deprecating. Their self-talk goes something like this: "Jesus died for such a worm as I. I am nothing. I am just a sinner saved by grace. I am still a dirty old man inside. If you knew the real me, you would not want anything to do with me. Neither would Jesus. So, what I must *do* in order to *be* what God wants me to *be* is to engage in self-denial and suppression of the real 'me' and my sin. I have to put myself down in self-surrender and brokenness. I have to 'die to self' in masochistic self-crucifixion. Basically I am bad, evil, and sinful, but 'praise the Lord,' my past is forgiven and the future is assured, even though the present is the 'pits'."

If that is all the typical evangelical Christian knows, and a "deeper life" teacher comes to explain to him that "as a Christian, you have 'Christ in you, the hope of glory'," that is "good news" indeed! It's almost like being "born again" again! And if someone comes to tell him that "Christ in you" means that you are "one spirit" with Jesus, and that you have a new spiritual identity in "union with Christ"—WOW—a whole new world of life and freedom opens up in understanding his "union-identity of being" by the indwelling Jesus.

In my own personal experience, it was the writings of W. Ian Thomas that first introduced me to the awareness of the indwelling Spirit of Christ, and it was Norman P. Grubb who filled out the dialectic understanding of an *identity union* with Christ.

Monistic Merging

In fairness, we must explain that there is another extreme in the opposite direction, when one fails to take into account the distinction of Christ and the Christian and over-emphasizes union to the point that it is no longer a "union" of two brought together but is regarded as a monistic oneness. Distinction is denied. Union is preempted.

The resultant premise of unitarian oneness posits that "God only" exists *in* all things and *as* all things. When God is viewed in such singularity as the only reality or person in the universe, the Christian understanding of the Trinitarian God is often sacrificed, and replaced with a God who is alleged to "be all in all." This premise of monistic and unitarian oneness is inevitably aligned with pantheistic concepts and the variant theses of panentheism. It is very similar to the foundational premises of many Eastern religions, as well as the teaching of Christian Science and the New Age Movement.

If God "is all in all," then all is one with God. This monistic pantheism implies a universalism wherein God is contained in all things and persons, and the "light" or "seed" of Christ is intrinsically present in all humanity. Such monistic universalism produces a divine determinism that denies human responsibility and the consequences of human choices, effectively denying Christian faith.

Those who have moved out of the dialectic of the tensioned balance of *distinction* and *union* with Christ often mistakenly attempt to portray their "God only" oneness in "union" terms. They may refer to an *organic union* between God and man, which they inaccurately liken to Christ's analogy of vine and branch. They may refer to *hypostatic union* of deity and humanity in the Christian, utilizing the terminology of the singularly unique Christological union of the God-man, Jesus. They often seek to explain that there is an "essential union" between the cosmic Christ and the Christian.

The Gnostic "knower" of God alleges himself to be mixed, merged, fused, or absorbed into coalescence with God. It is claimed that God and man are now equivalent and indistinguishable, united in the oneness of consubstantiation, i.e., of the same substance. Man is thus deified, divinized, or supernaturalized into godness, and regarded as intrinsically divine. Some within these circles blatantly declare, "I am God" or "I am Christ" or "I am the Spirit," and claim that everything Jesus said about Himself, they can now declare about themselves.

What does this do to the concept of humanity? If humanity is absorbed into deity, then humanity is essentially displaced, replaced, abandoned, dissolved, annihilated or obliterated. This reductionist depersonalizing of humanity within the absorption of the deification of humanity causes some to proclaim, "I am no longer human." "I am not; only He is." In such a thesis of obliteration and replacement, the "union of being" with Christ has been eschewed and jettisoned by failure to give due emphasis to the dialectic of *distinction* and *union* between Christ and the Christian.

The loss of tensioned dialectic facilitates a return to the Greek dualism that fostered docetism, the first heresy of the early church. Docetism asserted that

Jesus was not really human, but only "appeared" to be human, thus destroying the dialectic of deity and humanity in the Christological union. Those who advocate monistic merging perpetuate a variation of the docetic heresy in the claim that the Christian is "no longer human," but just "appears" to be human, while essentially divine.

As noted previously, Norman P. Grubb often reiterated the dialectic balance of *distinction* and *union* in his teaching and writing. Some representative quotations from his writings are contained in an addendum to this book (cf. page 83).

Chapter 6

Union of Doing

The "union of being" that recognizes the *distinction* of Christ's indwelling the Christian and the *union* of the Christian's identity with Christ must, of necessity, find actuation and experiential expression in the "union of doing" whereby the living Lord Jesus dynamically lives out His life in Christian behavior.

The "union of being" and the "union of doing," or more technically *ontological union* and *operational union*, can be considered as another dialectic, but this study will only observe them as the sequential follow-through from *being* to *doing*. In previous writings I have often used the phrase, "ontological dynamic." My intent in employing that phrase is to express that the Being (ontology) of God must find functional expression in the dynamic of His operational activity within and through the Christian's behavior.

God is an active God. It is the deistic perspective of God that views Him as a distant and detached deity not actively involved in the universe and in His people. The inherent attributes of God demand that He actively express Himself as the Love, Justice, Holiness, Savior, etc. that He *is*. God *does* what He *does*, because He *is* Who He *is*.

When the very Being of the Triune God has joined Himself to a receptive individual to become the basis of that person's Christian identity of "being," then He must be allowed to *act* as the God that He *is* in that Christian's behavior. In other words, it is imperative that the Christian *behave* like who he has *become* "in Christ" (in union with Christ).

This Christian behavior, however, is not a self-produced, self-generated, self-actuated activity whereby a Christian strives to succeed at the project of Christian living in accord with some proceduralized "how-to" formulas for doing what God expects.

----------------- ✳ -----------------

Just as our "union of being" was divinely initiated, the "union of doing" is also divinely actuated by the grace of God.

You cannot live the Christian life. *I* cannot live the Christian life. The Christian life is impossible, if conceived as the actions that a Christian must self-generate to "live like Jesus" and "love like Jesus."

But God is not interested in our "works" by which we might try to "measure up" and please Him. It was not our "works" which effected our "union of being" with Christ (Eph. 2:9; Rom. 3:28), and it will not be our "works" that facilitate the *doing* of Christian living.

The only One Who can live the Christian life is Jesus. He lived out the divine life perfectly in history, and now He wants to live out His life in, as, and through us.[2]

---------------- ✳ ----------------

All "good works" in the Christian life
are the outworking of His life and character.

"We are created in Christ Jesus for good works, which God prepared beforehand, that we should walk in them" (Eph. 2:10). God "equips us in every good thing to do His will, *working in us* that which is pleasing in His sight through Jesus Christ" (Heb. 13:21).

The Christian life is the "supplied life." The active provision for living the Christian life is supplied by the grace of God in Jesus Christ. The Christian, therefore, lacks nothing required to *be* and *do* all that God desires in him. Some have labeled this as "triumphalism," going so far as to declare, "It is too good to be true." On the contrary, God revealed

Himself to Paul, saying, "My grace is sufficient for you" (II Cor. 12:9), and Paul asserted, "I can do all things through Christ Who strengthens me" (Phil. 4:13).

When Paul wrote, "God is able to make all grace abound to you, that always having all sufficiency in everything, you may have an abundance for every good deed" (II Cor. 9:8), his statement was valid not only for Christian giving, but for the entirety of Christian living as well. We have all that is required to live the Christian life in the "union of doing" with the living Lord Jesus.

Trinitarian Action

The dynamic for the "union of doing" is provided in every Christian by the presence and provision of the entire Trinity—Father, Son, and Holy Spirit. "God is at work in us, both to will and to work for His good pleasure" (Phil. 2:13), Paul advised the Philippians. Those words of assurance directly followed the admonition to "work out your own salvation in fear and trembling" (Phil. 2:12), which emphasizes the distinction of personal responsibility.

To the Thessalonians Paul gave a list of admonitions (I Thess. 5:11-22), following it up with the assurance, "Faithful is He Who calls you, and He will also bring it to pass" (I Thess. 5:24).

God the Father is the dynamic for our "union of doing" in the Christian life. "Not that we are adequate in ourselves to consider anything as coming from ourselves, but our adequacy is from God" (II Cor. 3:5).

In like manner, God the Son is operating in Christians as the energizer and expresser of His life. "It is no longer I who lives, but Christ *lives* in me" (Gal. 2:20), Paul explained to the Galatians.

✷

It is not just that "Christ resides as an occupant in me," but that "Christ *lives* in me, as the dynamic expression of His life," Paul proclaimed.

"Having been reconciled, we shall be saved by His life" (Rom. 5:10), Paul wrote to the Romans, and this "saving life of Christ" is the means by which we are "made safe" from dysfunction in order to function as God intends, "reigning in life through Jesus Christ" (Rom. 5:17).

The very "life of Jesus is manifested in our mortal bodies" (II Cor. 4:10,11), because we have "the treasure (which is Christ) in these earthen vessels, that the surpassing greatness of the power may be of God, and not of ourselves" (II Cor. 4:7).

The living Lord Jesus is the dynamic of our "union of doing" in the Christian life.

Since "the Lord is the Spirit" (II Cor. 3:17), the "union of doing" is also attributable to the Christian's being "filled (or controlled) by the Spirit" (Eph. 5:18), in order that we might "walk by the Spirit" (Gal. 5:16,25) and "live by the Spirit" (Rom. 8:13). The Holy Spirit even serves as the pray-er in the Christian,[3] for "we do not know how to pray as we should" (Rom. 8:26). Likewise, we "worship in spirit and in truth" (John 4:24), as the Spirit of Christ is the worshipper[4] expressing the worth-ship of God's character in the "union of doing."

It is not necessary or advisable for Christians to attempt to analyze or evaluate how the Triune God is expressing His life in the "union of doing." Believing that we have a "union of being" with Christ, we can spontaneously *behave* like who we have *become* as Christ-ones. That is part of the "freedom for which Christ has set us free" (Gal. 5:1). We are free to *be* and *do* whatever Christ wants to *be* and *do* in, as, and through us.

Response-ability

In our Christian freedom we are also responsible to allow for the divine dynamic of the "union of doing." It is here that we commence to observe the necessary *distinction* that balances the *union* of divine action.

48

God created humans as choosing creatures, and since our humanness is not displaced or dissolved when we are joined in "union of being" with Christ as Christians, the Christian remains responsible for his choices.

If we view our responsibility as the *"response-ability"* to make behavioral choices of faith that allow Christ to live His life and energize the "union of doing" in our behavioral expression, we can avoid falling into a works-oriented system of religion performance.

Jesus' discourse about the vine and the branches in John 15 is often used to explain the Christian's "union with Christ." It is not *organic union* that Jesus is teaching, but a balanced perspective of *union* and *distinction* in the "union of doing." "Apart from Me, you can do nothing" (John 15:5), Jesus declared.

Legitimate exegesis does not allow us to isolate the phrase, "you can do nothing," and emphasize a totally divine expression. The entire analogy of vine and branches refers not to essential "union of being," but to the functional expression of divine activity in the Christian. Observe the distinction of pronouns in the complete verse: "*I* am the vine, *you* are the branches; *he* who abides in *Me*, and *I* in *him*, *he* bears much fruit, for apart from *Me*, *you* can do nothing" (John 15:5).

✻

What is the Christian's responsibility?
To "abide in Christ" (John 15:5-7).

What does it mean to "abide"? The word means "to reside, to settle in, to make yourself at home." The Christian is to make himself at home *in Christ* (in union with Christ), to settle in and live there. That does not involve any "works" of performance, but it does involve a responsible decision of abiding faith. In his first epistle John wrote, "If what you heard from the beginning abides in you, you also will abide in the Son and in the Father" (I John 2:24).

The response-ability of the Christian is the choice of faith. Faith is not just believing or assenting to correct data. Nor is faith the conjuring up of enough trust to rely on Christ. Faith is a constant choosing of receptivity to God's activity, a continuous availability to God's ability.

As noted earlier, our "union of being" is a derived identity, and in the "union of doing" we continue our human function of derivative, dependent, and contingent faith. Paul explained to the Colossians, "As you received Christ Jesus the Lord (by faith), so walk in Him, ...established in your faith" (Col. 2:6,7). The Christian life is lived only by the grace-dynamic of God's action, received by faith.

Paul's references to the "obedience of faith" (Rom. 1:5; 16:26) seem to indicate that Christian obedience is composed of faith. Christian obedience is not to be viewed within the legal paradigm of strenuous striving to keep the rules and regulations of the Law, but is simply to be understood as "listening under" (Greek word *hupakouo*) God to ascertain the next situation where we can be receptive to His activity in and through us.

James' statements become all the more meaningful when we understand faith as Christian receptivity to divine activity. "Faith without works is useless" (James 2:20) and "dead" (James 2:17,26), James writes. If there is no consequent outworking of divine activity, then it can safely be surmised that there was not faith-receptivity to God's activity, i.e., whatever "faith" was alleged, it was useless, dead, non-existent or false because it did not allow for the receptivity of the outworking of divine activity.

Grace is "God in action," *doing* what He *does* because He *is* Who He *is*, and our responsibility is to be receptive in faith to allow Him to *be* and *do* what He wants to *be* and *do* in us, in the "union of doing."

Chapter 7

Christian Expression

What about all of the imperative action-commands that are stated throughout the New Testament? Someone counted more than one thousand (1,000!) imperative verbs in the New Testament.

The Concept of "Commandments"

The *distinction* between Christ and the Christian seems to loom so large when we consider the concept of "commandments." Didn't Jesus say, "He who has My commandments and keeps them, he it is who loves Me" (John 14:21)? Yes, but Jesus did not command anything that He is not willing to keep and perform in our "union of doing." He is the *dynamic* of all of His own *demands*.

Within the new covenant concept of grace, *imperatives* are always based on *indicatives*. The indicative statements of God's presence and sufficiency are always the foundation for the fulfillment of the imperative action verbs.

——————— ✳ ———————

Christ does not ask anything of us
that He is not willing to fulfill
in our "union of doing."

As noted previously, Paul's admonition to "work out your own salvation with fear and trembling" (Phil. 2:12) is an *imperative*. The *indicative* statement is, "God is at work in you both to will and to work for His good pleasure" (Phil. 2:13).

Another *imperative* is, "Do not worry about anything" (Phil. 4:6). The following *indicative* is, "I can do all things through Christ Who strengthens me" (Phil. 4:13).

"Rejoice always, pray without ceasing, …abstain from every form of evil" (I Thess. 5:16,17,22) are the *imperatives*. "Faithful is He Who calls you, and He will bring it to pass" (I Thess. 5:24) is the foundational *indicative*.

"Love one another" (John 13:34,35) was Jesus' command. The supply for such is indicated in that "the love of God is shed abroad in our hearts by the Holy Spirit Who has been given to us" (Rom. 5:5).

The *imperative* is, "Be strong in the Lord" (Eph. 6:12), but the *indicative* awareness is that this is "in the strength of His might" (Eph. 6:12), for we are strong only "by the strength which God supplies" (I Pet. 4:11).

"Let this mind be in you which was in Christ Jesus" (Phil. 2:5), Paul commanded the Philippians, and to the Colossians he wrote, "Set your minds on things above" (Col. 3:2); but he advised the Corinthians, "We have the mind of Christ" (I Cor. 2:16).

"Discipline yourself unto godliness" (I Tim. 4:7) was the admonition to Timothy, but Peter indicates, "His divine power has granted us everything pertaining to life and godliness" (II Pet. 1:3).

✱

The *imperatives* are always based on the *indicatives* of God's grace in Christ, and are never commands for self-produced behavioral "works" of righteousness.

Many of the imperative verbs demand action that cannot possibly be construed as "work," but only as a faith-choice. As noted above, "to abide" is simply to "settle in, stay put, and make oneself at home" in Christ Jesus (in union with Christ Jesus). To "reckon yourselves dead unto sin" (Rom. 6:11) is to "count it as a fact" that you were crucified with Christ and are "alive unto God in Christ Jesus (in union with Christ Jesus)" (Rom. 6:11). To "present your bodies a living sacrifice" (Rom. 12:1) and "your members as members of righteousness" (Rom. 6:13) is simply to hand yourself over to God in surrender. These imperatives simply reveal that the Christian is obliged to be receptive in faith to the union-activity of Christ in the Christian.

When we are receptive in faith to allow the living Christ to be the ontological dynamic whereby He manifests His own life in our behavior, there are two general areas of Christian expression. We must emphasize again that these are not to be regarded as criteria by which one might measure Christian maturity or success.

As we spontaneously allow Jesus Christ to re-present His life in us, He will inevitably manifest His *character* and His *ministry* in the "union of doing" that we call the "Christian life." In other words, Christ will *be* and *do* what He desires to uniquely *be* and *do* in each of us.

Character

The divine character of Christ is expressed as the "fruit of the Spirit." "The fruit of the Spirit is love, joy, peace, patience, kindness, goodness, faithfulness, gentleness, and godly control of oneself" (Gal. 5:22,23). These always come in one cluster, for together they are the character of Christ, and should not be severed from one another for independent acquisition or development.

When a Christians says, "What I need is more patience…or more kindness…" one might respond, "Do you not have Christ? He is our patience. He is our kindness. He is our joy. He is our peace. …etc." We do not need something more than Jesus. He is everything to us in the Christian life. Our only need and response-ability is to allow Him to experientially express Himself in the "union of doing."

As we "abide" and "make ourselves at home" *in Christ*, we "bear much fruit" (John 15:5). Notice that the verse does not say we "*produce* much fruit," but rather, that we "*bear*" the "fruit of goodness and righteousness" (Phil. 1:11; Heb. 12:11) and "truth" (Eph. 5:9), and in so doing we "walk in a manner worthy of the Lord, pleasing Him in all respects, bearing fruit in every good work" (Col. 1:10).

---

*

The character fruit of Christ
that is inclusive of all expressions is
divine love.

Love is the first character trait mentioned as "the fruit of the Spirit" (Gal. 5:22), and Paul explained that "faith working through love" (Gal. 5:6) fulfills the entire intent of the Law (Gal. 5:14; Rom. 13:8-10). "God *is* Love" (John 4:8,16), the apostle John twice states, and when we express His character of love in the union-doing of our Christian lives, we are manifesting the intimate heart of God for *others*.

————————— ✳ —————————

Love is always *other*-oriented,
in contrast to the natural self-orientation of man.

——————————————————

The divine character of love can be derived only from God by faith, which is why John wrote, "Everyone who loves is born of God and knows God" (I John 4:7). "If we love one another, God abides in us, and His love is perfected in us" (I John 4:12).

"Having all things pertaining to life and godliness" (II Pet. 1:3), the "mystery of godliness" (I Tim. 3:16) is revealed as we "desire to live godly in Christ Jesus (in union with Christ Jesus)" (II Tim. 3:12). Godliness cannot be generated by man's performance, but is always and exclusively the expression of the character of God in man.

The holy character of God that is set apart from all others has come to dwell in the Christian in Christ Jesus (I Cor. 1:30). "God is holy" (Isa. 6:3) and Jesus is the "Holy One of God" (Luke 4:34; Acts 2:27), having "called us with a holy calling" (II Tim. 1:9)

"that we might share His holiness" (Heb. 12:10).
"God has called us for the purpose of sanctification"
(II Thess. 4:7) that we should be "set apart" to
function as He intended, in the manifestation of His
holy character unto His own glory.

Ministry

In like manner as the *character of Christ* is
expressed in the "fruit of the Spirit," so the *ministry
of Christ* is expressed by the grace-gifts of the Spirit.
The *charismata*,[5] the grace-expressions of the Spirit
of Christ in the Christian (Rom. 12:6-8; I Cor. 12:1-
31), are the means of Christian ministry (Eph. 4:11-
13).

These so-called "spiritual gifts" are not
specialized job descriptions or trophies of spirituality.
They are simply the expressive means by which the
Spirit of Christ serves others in the new covenant
"ministry of the Spirit" (II Cor. 3:6,8), the "ministry
of reconciliation" (II Cor. 5:18).

Christian ministry is not the actions we engage in
to "serve Jesus," since "God is not served by human
hands, as though He needed anything" (Acts 17:25).
Rather, Christian ministry is the outflow and
overflow of Jesus' love for others, in the Christian
"union of doing."

Barnabas and Paul returned to Jerusalem to
report what "*God had done through them* among the
Gentiles" (Acts 15:12). To the Romans, Paul

explained, "I do not presume to speak of anything except what *Christ has accomplished through me*...in the power of the Spirit" (Rom. 15:18,19). In his epistle to the Ephesians, Paul wrote, "I was made a minister, according to the gift of God's grace which was given to me *according to the working of His power*" (Eph. 3:7).

In the context of ministry giftedness, Peter exhorts Christians, "Whoever serves, let him do so *by the strength which God supplies*; so that in all things God may be glorified through Jesus Christ" (I Pet. 4:10,11).

———————— ✳ ————————

Legitimate Christian ministry
must be Christ's action
in the "union of doing" of our Christian lives.

Thus we serve as "ambassadors for Christ" (II Cor. 5:20), desirous that people be reconciled to God and to one another. As priests (I Pet. 2:9; Rev. 1:6), we minister to others and re-present God. As witnesses (Acts 1:8), we lay down our lives for others. (The Greek word for "witness" is *marture*, the etymological root of the English word "martyr.") The Christian becomes a praying and living intercessor for others, for Christ "always lives to make intercession" (Heb. 7:25) before God and for others.

As we minister in the "union of doing" with Christ, evangelism is not a propagational task we perform in order to win the world to Christ, but is the spontaneous expression of Christ shared "as you are going" (Matt. 28:19) through life, thereby allowing the living Christ to "draw all men to Himself" (John 12:32), that they, too, might become disciples and Christ-expressers. Saint Francis of Assisi is reported to have said, "Share Christ wherever you go, and if you have to – use words."

Collective Union

Much of Christian ministry is within and in conjunction with the collective body of Christ, the church (I Cor. 12:27; Eph. 1:22,23; Col. 1:18,24). Christians should not engage in a "lone ranger" individualism that fails to recognize the corporate church union that we have with Christ, the head of the body (Col. 1:18; Eph. 1:22).

Many who have emphasized personal and subjective "union with Christ" through the ages have lacked a meaningful understanding of ecclesiology, the doctrine of the church of Jesus Christ. Christians are *in Christ* (in union with Christ) together with one another, and must be "united in spirit" (Phil. 2:2) in a "one spirit" (Phil. 1:27) "unity of the Spirit" (Eph. 4:3) that recognizes their mutual oneness (John 17:21,22).

The "unity of doing" expression of our "union with Christ" encompasses our interactive function as "members" (Rom. 12:5; I Cor. 12:12-27) of the body of Christ. In the church community we appreciate our "common unity" in Christ and enjoy the fellowship and communion (common union) with Christ together, allowing the interpersonal and relational oneness of Father, Son, and Holy Spirit to produce harmony and unity as we "love one another" (John 13:34,35; I Thess. 4:9; Heb. 13:1; I Pet. 1:22; I John 3:23; 4:7-21).

———————— ✳ ————————

In our "unity of doing" with Christ,
we need each other!
Christ in me desires to love and cooperate
with Christ in you!

Mutual encouragement (Heb. 10:24,25) is particularly important when we experience the testing (John 6:6; Heb. 11:17; James 1:3) and temptations (I Cor. 10:13; I Thess. 3:5; II Pet. 2:9) of the trials (James 1:2) of life.

Our "union with Christ" is tested when we are tempted to doubt that we are who we are in the "union of being" with Christ. In like manner, we are tempted to question that our actions in the "union of doing" are of any consequence or significance, rather than "seeing through" the situation to recognize

God's opportunities to manifest the life of Jesus, regardless of how tough the going gets. God's opportunities may even involve the privilege of "suffering with Christ" (Rom. 8:17) in the "fellowship of His sufferings" (Phil. 3:10), whereby we "fill up what is lacking in Christ's afflictions" (Col. 1:24), allowing the living Lord Jesus to continue to experience the pain and sufferings of the world's assaults in our bodies and in His body, the church.

Sinful Misrepresentation

In the midst of the temptations and trials of life, we may lose perspective of our union sufficiency in Christ. Despite our knowing that we are "new creatures" (II Cor. 5:17) who are "complete in Christ" (Col. 2:10) and "one spirit (with Him)" (I Cor. 6:17), our failure to spiritually appraise (I Cor. 2:11-16) our "union with Christ" can result in an operational distinction that chooses to act in a manner that misrepresents who we are *in Christ* (in union with Christ). When we do so, it can be said that we are "not acting like ourselves," not manifesting the character of Christ, and thus "missing the mark" of God's intent and desire to express Himself in us, and as us, and through us at all times; *i.e.,* we have sinned.

"Whatever is not of faith is sin" (Rom. 14:23). Whatever is not receptive of God's activity is sinful misrepresentation. Was it Christ in us who sinned?

May it never be! Christ cannot and does not sin in our "union of doing," so sinful expression evidences that in the *distinction* of our *union* we exercised our freedom of choice to act contrary to our spiritual identity and Christ's character. Does this alter who we are in our spiritual "union of being" with Christ? Definitely not! Our spiritual identity with Christ is secure, in spite of our sinful misrepresentation. How, then, should we respond to such sinful expression in our lives? It is our privilege to draw nigh unto God with a repentant heart: "If we confess our sins, He is faithful and just to forgive us our sins and to cleanse us from all unrighteousness" (I John 1:9).

An understanding of "union with Christ" should not produce a perfectionism that asserts, "Christians cannot sin." Let it be clearly stated, though, that this is not to maintain that Christians must sin, or will inevitably sin.

$$*$$

In our "union of being" and "union of doing"
with Christ, we have everything necessary
to manifest righteousness and avoid sinfulness.

Again, Jesus Christ in us does not sin! This is not to say that the Christian "cannot sin," but that the Christian "can...not sin" as he remains receptive to Christ's righteous character within him. The assertion that we are making is that it is "possible not to sin" as the Christian operates by faith and manifests the Christ-life, but we must not claim that it is "not possible for the Christian to sin."

The apostle John addressed this issue in his first epistle, stating, "If we say (as they, the Gnostic perfectionists, say) that 'we have no sin,' we are deceiving ourselves, and the truth is not in us" (I John 1:8). "If we say (as they, the Gnostic elitists, say) that 'we have not sinned' ('because we have union with Christ'), we make Him a liar, and His word is not in us" (I John 3:10). "But if (when) anyone sins, we have an Advocate with the Father, Jesus Christ the Righteous..." (I John 2:1).

When the Christian is joined to the Lord at regeneration in a "new creature" union, "old things are passed away, and all things become new" (II Cor. 5:17) spiritually. *Distinction* becomes evident, though, when the Christian recognizes and admits that there are idiosyncratic patterns of selfishness and sinfulness within the desires of his soul. Paul refers to these patterned desires of the soul as "the desires of the flesh" (Gal. 5:16; Eph. 2:3), and urges Christians to "make no provision for the flesh in regard to its desires" (Rom. 13:14). A functional antagonism of behavioral conflict is staged in the soul as "the flesh sets its desire against the Spirit, and the Spirit against the flesh, for these are in opposition to one another" (Gal. 5:17).

The Christian must remember that his *union-identity* with Christ is a spiritual reality in the spirit of man. *Distinction* is experienced in our soul and body—the psychological and physiological function—when the Christian fails to "set his mind on the Spirit" (Rom. 8:5,6), and instead "sets his mind on the flesh" (Rom. 8:5,6,7) in response to temptation. This need not be!

_____ ✱ _____

The Christian is no longer "in the flesh"
(in union with the Evil One who patterned those
selfish and sinful patterns of fleshly desires),
but "in the Spirit"
(in union with the Spirit of Christ),
as Paul states in Romans 8:8,9.

_____

"Walking according to the flesh" (Rom. 8:4), "living according to the flesh" (Rom. 8:12,13), is a misrepresentation of who we are in Christ.

Chapter 8

Evangelical Performance

When the Christian's "union of doing" in Christ is neglected or denied, and when the distinction of faithful responsibility is over-emphasized, the resultant extremism of human potentiality creates an emphasis on man's doing and performance of religious "works."

Failing to take into account that the Christian's "adequacy is from God" (II Cor. 3:5), and that Jesus said, "Apart from Me, you can do nothing" (John 15:5), much of contemporary evangelical "Christian religion" has reverted to the fallacious thesis of self-generated righteous behavior in accord with codified behavioral standards (cf. Gal. 2:21). They employ such phrases as, "Do your best, and God will do the rest," or "God helps those who help themselves," often thinking that these are biblical injunctions. These are not biblical concepts; in fact, they are contrary to the new covenant concept of God's grace in Jesus Christ functioning as the dynamic of the Christian's "union of doing" with Christ.

Performance incentives have become the motivational focus of most evangelical preaching. Christians are urged to act in ways that are acceptable and pleasing to God, despite the fact that "Christ accepted us to the glory of God" (Rom. 15:7), and we are "accepted in the Beloved" (Eph. 1:6, KJV). Active striving to be perfect is often encouraged, whereas Christians have already been made perfect (Phil. 3:15; Heb. 12:23) and need only be receptive in faith to the expression of God's perfect character in their Christian behavior.

Trying to "be like Jesus" in a conformational Christ-likeness that imitates Jesus' example is a common theme in popular evangelical teaching.

———————— ✳ ————————

It is not copycat imitation of Jesus
that God desires, but that the
"life of Jesus might be manifested in our
mortal bodies" (II Cor. 4:10)—
manifestation, rather than imitation!

The issue is not "what would Jesus do?" but "wanting/watching what Jesus does."

Calls for commitment, consecration, and dedication are laced throughout most contemporary exhortations in the churches today. It is not personal commitment to performance that God desires of

Christians, but that they might "submit themselves to God" (James 4:7) and thus to all that He is committed to *be* and *do* in, as, and through them.

Seeking to discover and do the "will of God" is another performance pursuit of popular religion, as they fail to understand that the "will of God" is always Jesus—His life lived out in His people in every situation.

The Never-ending Treadmill

The treadmill of performance is never-ending! Christians are admonished to pray more, to read their Bibles more, to be more involved in church activities. Churches employ guilt-producing incentives to manipulate people to behave in such a way as to have a "good testimony" and to engage in the pressurized evangelistic procedures of active witnessing for Jesus. People are even encouraged to "serve the Lord" in the ecclesiastical programs of church ministry until they "burn out for Jesus."

"God is not served by human hands, as though He needed anything" (Acts 17:25), Paul said in Athens.

Whereas "religion" advocates "performance service," the gospel of grace in Jesus Christ recognizes that Christians are "available servants" of Christ who function by the "union of doing" with Christ.

Christians who operate by the
inexhaustible grace of God
will never "burn out."

_____

When the dynamic "union of doing" in Christ is
turned into performance expectations, then
Christianity (Christ-in-you-ity) has degenerated into
religious exercise. Christianity is not religion![6]

The word "religion" is etymologically derived
from the Latin words *religare* and *religio*, meaning
"to bind, tie, or attach." Religion ties people to the
believe-right doctrines and teachings of
fundamentalistic belief-systems.[7] Religion attaches
people to social organizations and denominations
with hierarchical control.[8] Religion binds people to
the legalistic keeping of rules and regulations of
behavioral laws and codes of conduct. Christianity is
not "religion."

Likewise, many people have been deceived into
thinking that Christianity is the advocacy of
morality,[9] that educates people in character values so
they might behave in ethical conformity. This is
another denial of the Christian's "union of doing" in
Christ by which the life and character of Christ is
lived out in Christian behavior to the glory of God.
But the evangelical do-right religion persists in the
utopian dream that social activism for the purpose of

ethical consensus will solve the problems of the society in which we live.[10]

The religion of performance does not foster "the peace that passes understanding" (Phil. 4:7) in an "assurance of understanding" (Col. 2:2), "faith" (Heb. 10:22), and "hope" (Heb. 6:11). The freedom (Gal. 5:1,13) and liberty (II Cor. 3:17) of spontaneous expression of Christ's life and action are quenched in the performance expectations that produce fear, insecurity, paranoia, and resignation.

Works-oriented Christians, never sure that they have done enough for Jesus, are always fearful (cf. I John 4:18) that their performance is inadequate. "Not that we are adequate to consider anything as coming from ourselves, but our adequacy is of God" (II Cor. 3:5). Despite the "once saved, always saved" eternal security doctrines in some evangelical churches, the majority of Christians experience an inevitable insecurity about the performance of their behavior and service, which often leads to doubts concerning their regeneration.

Some Christians become paranoid about what they are supposed to do, engaging in an equivocating questioning, "Is it me, or is it Jesus, that wants to do this?" Others just resign themselves to misrepresentation, declaring, "I can't help but sin. I'm only human," effectively denying their union of being and doing in Christ. Genuine Christians, however, cannot sin with indifference or impunity. The living Christ within them will not let them get away with it.

Granted, there are those who engage in the hypocrisy of attempting to *impress* others of their "spirituality," but most performance-oriented Christians are seeking to *repress* or *suppress* their sin inclinations and propensities by pushing them below the surface of their behavioral "acting out."

Many *obsess* in a sin-consciousness that focuses more on their sinfulness than on the living Christ Whom they have received (cf. Heb. 12:2). Via navel-gazing introspection, these Christians seek to *assess* their progress of performance as gauged by the religious standards of spiritual success, but they continue to be overwhelmed by guilt, shame, and condemnation for their sin. They repeatedly respond to the "altar call" to *confess* their sins and seek God's forgiveness for failure to perform what God never expected them to perform in the first place.

———————— ✳ ————————

God's desire is simply that the Christian be
receptive and available
to *express* the character of Christ.

———————————————————

The institutional church, meanwhile, is guilty of keeping Christians on the treadmill of do-right religion. Guilt and condemnation are intense psychological motivators that keep people involved and attending the church services, where they continue to confess their sins, plead for God's forgiveness and help in prayer, and give generously to "the Lord's work." In return, they experience an emotional and sensate ecstasy, which they call "worship," which temporarily masks the sin-consciousness of their inadequate performance, and induces them to dedicate and commit themselves to better performance. A cyclical pattern of mutually self-serving activity, indeed!

Deterministic Inevitability

Though less common, the opposite extreme— i.e., denying the *distinction* of Christian responsibility and pushing *union* with Christ's action to the point of a unified inevitability of divine action—also destroys the tensioned balance of the Christian's "union of doing."

The misemphasis of a "monistic merging" in the Christian's "union of being" becomes a "deterministic inevitability" when applied to the Christian's "union of doing."

The dynamic of the divine activity of Father, Son, and Holy Spirit, without the *distinction* of human responsibility, disallows any real sense of *union* and results in a mechanistic oneness that loses or repudiates the personal relationalism of the Christian's "union with Christ."

If the essential equivalence of deification is advocated as the explanation of Christian union, and

"He is me, and I am He," then it follows that "whatever I do is what He does," and "everything I do is Christ in action, even though it may not appear to be so to others."

Such a deterministic expression of divine action within the Christian produces a fatalistic denial of responsibility which has led some to declare, "God doesn't mean for man to have faith, but just to be the inevitable God-expresser that he is." According to this thesis, the Christian, as a passive instrument of automatic divine action, just "goes with the flow" of divine inevitability, and the Christian life becomes a non-participatory autopilot experience of just being the channel or conduit of Christ's action.

Consistently, the thesis of absorption into God and the obliteration of humanness should lead to the nirvanic nihilism of nothingness, but such is not the case for those who tout their acquiescence to the direct-drive of divine expression. They are prone to well up with the pride of Gnostic elitism, claiming to be spiritual "knowers" and "see-ers" with advanced spiritual perception and God-consciousness.

Despite their claims of a consubstantial coalescence with Christ, their distinct egocentricity is revealed in their assertions, "I do what I will, for what I will is what He wills, since He is my willed activity." On this assumption (or presumption) of deity-identity, such spiritualizers claim to speak the "word of faith" and creatively "call into being what was not, or call what is not, 'is'." Contrary to the biblical concept of faith as "our receptivity of God's activity," they indicate that "faith is just speaking your word" as the God-person that you are, and thus functioning as co-creator, co-god, co-redeemer, co-savior in fused oneness with the divine. This is no longer the "union of doing" of a relational "union with Christ," but is the presumptive arrogance of an indistinguishable deity expression.

Unconcerned about the *distinction* of sinful misrepresentation, the extreme oneness advocates argue, "Christ cannot sin. Christ is the 'new man' in me. Therefore, I cannot sin." In direct parallel with the nascent Gnostic thinking of Asia Minor towards the end of the first century, they declare, "We have no sin" (I John 3:8), and "We have not sinned" (I John 3:10).

Behavioral incongruities are justified and explained away as mere "appearances" (trace of docetism) incorrectly perceived by those who are not pure God-see-ers who can "see God in everything." "What appears to be sin is but an illusion; sin is nothing," is their mantra. What is this, but the delusion of libertine antinomianism that disregards the divine expression of God's holy behavior, and flaunts their alleged liberty to sin by becoming a "law unto themselves"?

The apostle Paul was aghast at such thinking. "Shall we sin to our heart's content and see how far we can exploit the grace of God? What a ghastly thought" (Rom. 6:1, JBP).

Collective union with Christ in the body of Christ, the church, is eschewed by the individualistic spiritualists. Prayer and worship are regarded as irrelevant and unnecessary. "Since we are one with God, why pray to ourselves? Why worship ourselves?" is their reasoning. What they call "ministry" is often a condescending (and sometimes deceitful) attempt to raise others' awareness and consciousness of the cosmic and universal monistic oneness.

Conclusion

Neither deistic detachment nor monistic merging allow for the balanced dialectic tension of *union* and *distinction* that are required in a biblical understanding of "union with Christ." It is of utmost importance that Christians in every age understand both their "union of being" and "union of doing" in Christ in accord with the biblical data and Jesus' declaration, "I am the vine, you are the branches...Apart from Me, you can do nothing" (John 15:5).

In commencing our study of both the "union of being" and the "union of doing," we presented careful and thorough biblical documentation for the ontological and operational "union with Christ." It is always important to note the biblical documentation for the *distinction* involved in "union with Christ," for it is we, human creatures, who are joined in a real union to the Lord, Jesus Christ, and apart from the *distinction* of the two being joined together there is no real *union*.

But the more one emphasizes the *distinction* of man's responsibility, the more there begins to be a shift away from the Christocentric focus towards a more anthropocentric perspective. If the emphasis on *distinction* is pushed to concepts of separation and detachment that abandon the recognition of *union*, then the anthropocentric becomes humanism— humanism dressed in the garb of "Christian religion," i.e., "evangelical humanism."[11]

On the other hand, any concept of "union with Christ" that loses sight of the biblical balance of *distinction* can cause *union* to be lost in the monistic merging of Gnosticism and pantheism. The biblical balance must be maintained, and we must maintain the dialectic tension of "union with Christ."

---

*

If our theology does not begin with and maintain a
focus on Who Christ *is* and what Christ *does*,
then it soon degenerates into thoughts and practices
that glorify man rather than God.

The starting point must be the divine action of *union* with Christ.

The popular evangelicalism that pervades the Western expression of "Christian religion" today has such a minimal understanding of union and such a deistic emphasis on the detached separation of Christ and the Christian, that they do not even appear to be "in the ballpark" of a balanced biblical understanding of "union with Christ" which comprises the gospel of Jesus Christ. At the same time, Eastern philosophical concepts are gaining popularity in the West, and the resultant monistic unitarianism, often referred to as "New Age spirituality," is equally outside of the biblical balance of "union with Christ."

It is important to remember that the Western mind chafes at the balanced tension of dialectic. Western man seeks to push his thought into categories that end up being static systems of closed extremism.

Rare is the Christian who will respond to the constant direction of the Spirit of Christ and open-mindedly allow for the tension of *union* and *distinction*. When one emphasis is made, he says, "Yes, but…" When the other emphasis is made, he says, "Yes, but…" The "Yes, but…" exchanges are healthy within the tensioning balance of dialectic. The problem comes when people want to push the "Yes, but…" outside of the interaction of *union* and *distinction*, and thus advocate what is not biblical and not Christian, but rather an aberrant construct of man.

Allow me to conclude with this warning: The Christian who attempts to maintain a tensioned balance of *union* and *distinction*, refusing to "camp out" on one side or the other, will constantly be accused of dancing the "spiritual two-step" in a wishy-washy waffling that refuses to take a static stand in one camp or the other.

The dynamic of the dialectic balance of "union with Christ" will always be impossible to "pin down" in a system of thought, for Jesus Christ lives in each Christian as a unique and novel expression of Himself.

———————— ✳ ————————

Endnotes

1 Fowler, James A., *Three Divine Onenesses*. Fallbrook: CIY Publishing. 2002.
2 Fowler, James A., *Christ in us, Christ as us, Christ through us*. Fallbrook: CIY Publishing. 2001.
3 Fowler, James A., *Christocentric Prayer*. Fallbrook: CIY Publishing. 1994.
4 Fowler, James A., *Christocentric Worship*. Fallbrook: CIY Publishing. 1994.
5 Fowler, James A., *Charismata: Rethinking the So-called Spiritual Gifts*. Fallbrook: CIY Publishing. 1997.
6 Fowler, James A., *Christianity is NOT Religion*. Fallbrook: CIY Publishing. 1995.
7 Fowler, James A., *Christianity is NOT a Belief-system*. Fallbrook: CIY Publishing. 1994. Fowler, James A., Ch*ristianity is NOT Epistemology*. Fallbrook: CIY Publishing. 1993. Fowler, James A., *Christianity is NOT an Ideological Option*. Fallbrook: CIY Publishing. 2002.
8 Fowler, James A., *Christianity is NOT an ...ism*. Fallbrook: CIY Publishing. 1996.
9 Fowler, James A., *Christianity is NOT Morality*. Fallbrook: CIY Publishing. 1993.

10 Fowler, James A., *Christianity is NOT Problem-solving.* Fallbrook: CIY Publishing. 1997.
11 Fowler, James A., *Evangelical Humanism.* Fallbrook: CIY Publishing. 1990.

All of these writings are available for free downloading on the Christ In You website:
www.christinyou.net

Addendum

Quotations from the writings of Norman P. Grubb
on *union* and *distinction*.

The Liberating Secret - ©1955

14 - The Father and the Son dwell in us. Union, yet
distinctiveness, joined in one.

16 - It is the life of union, the one with The Other,
distinct from each other, yet one in each other,
interpenetrating.

22 - ...spirits unite. They interpenetrate. One dwells
in another. ...Both a union and a distinction between
them at the same time.

39 - ...his human spirit had one marvelous
potentiality; it could be the container of the Divine
Spirit via the tree of life, and yet not lose its own
individuality in being so; but that the two can dwell
together, each in the other, in an eternal fruitful bond
of union, the human being the delighted and loving
bond slave of the Divine.

The Deep Things of God - ©1958

9 - Creatures are created to *contain* the life, not to be
it in themselves: the essence of idolatry is to claim to
be what only God is. ...God can never give His own
godhead to another. ...Containers are not the thing in
itself.

10 - ...man can freely, intelligently, delightedly *contain* the living God, so that God lives His own divine life out through the living agency and co-operation of a human personality; but the human being never advances one iota beyond being a mere container of God for time and eternity.

11 - ...the human self is forever a container, a co-operator, a manifestor, but never the One in Himself.

36 - "the new I is Christ in me." ... He can only make creatures to contain Him. He cannot make other gods who are self-existent, ...for then He would cease to be God alone.

The Key to Everything - ©1960

23 - Now get this clear: the vessel never becomes the liquid, nor the liquid the vessel. I add this because we humans are so proud that there creeps into us the idea that we can be deified. That is blasphemy. There is no such thing as self-deification, except that of Satan, the pseudo-God, and what we share with him. The divine can dwell in the human, but forever the human is the human and the divine the divine. God has said, "I will not give my glory to another."

24,25 - That is the vital importance of the vessel illustration: we are forever the container; He is that which we contain. That relationship never changes.

Jesus gave us the vine and branches illustration. Through this our eyes are opened to the secret of the universe: union – the mystery of the universe: how two can be one and yet remain two. ...The living God, the living Christ, and I actually become one person and function as one person. Separation is impossible. It has disappeared. We function entirely and forever and naturally as one person. And yet we remain two!

God Unlimited - ©1962

87 - ...being real humans, we must accept our humanity. We are God's means of entry into the human situation, even as Jesus in the flesh was.
158 - ...carefully preserve the fact that neither Christ nor we lose our distinct identity through eternity, He God, we man; it is never a relationship of total absorption where man ceases to be redeemed man, or Christ ceases to be God the Son.

The Spontaneous You - ©1966

54 - ...we are vessels forever, we the creature, He the Creator, neither one ever becoming the other, nor mixing in that sense.

Who Am I? - ©1974

95 - ...normal Christian living...is this 'mysterious' combination of the duality in the unity, the Positive and negative which alone makes manifestation of the Positive possible. It forever remains a duality in the unity, the Positive remains the Positive, the negative remains the negative; the one never becomes the other, the creature never becomes the Creator, or the son the Father, or the human the Deity.

90 - "we are called "vessels." A vessel is there only to contain. It does not become what it contains. The cup does not become the coffee, nor the coffee the cup.

97 - This does not mean that we are like two people separate within myself. No, we are one. I am "joined to the Lord—one spirit" (I Cor. 6:17); we are two, yet we are one. He is the One living in me, yet not as separate from me, but reproducing Himself by me—as vine through branch, head through body, husband through wife.

In our conscious union relationship: though each Christian is the two united in one, we don't see ourselves as thinking, speaking, acting, but it is He expressed through our forms... not I, but He living in me. That is the union-duality! We are two, but no, we are one...

132 - ...we are human selves, and our oneness with Christ does not alter our two-ness in being He and I. God's whole purpose is to express Himself through our fully human selves, just as He did with Jesus.

Union with Christ Diagram #1

Ontological

Distinction ←————

Balanced Tension ←————

Evangelical Detachment

Evangelicalism emphasizes
"doing" rather than "being"
Deistic concept of God -
detached and separated.
Transcendence instead of
immanence.
"God's up in heaven;
I am here on earth."

Objectification

God in heaven is angry.
Jesus tries to appease.
Jesus died for sins of man.
Jesus went to heaven to
convince Father to impute
benefits of His death to man
God willing to "declare righteous" and grant new status,
standing, and position.
Christian has ambiguous
"relationship" with Christ.

Double-minded Duality

Two natures in conflict.
Schizophrenic identity.
Paranoid motivations.
Doubts of salvation.
Emotional experientialism.

Concept of "Self"

Self-denigrating/deprecating
"Just a sinner saved by grace"
"Still a dirty old man"
Self-denial; suppression
Self-surrender, brokenness
Self-crucifixion, "Die to self"

Christ and the Christian

"If any man does not have the Spirit of Christ,
he is none of His" - Rom. 8:9
"The Spirit bears witness with our spirit, that
we are children of God" - Rom. 8:16
"...the life I now live in the flesh, I live by
faith in the Son of God" - Gal. 2:20b

Analogies

vessel/contents analogy - II Cor. 4:7
branch/vine analogy - Jn. 15:3-5
house/occupant analogy - II Cor. 5:1
temple/god analogy - I Cor. 3:16; 6:19
body/head analogy - I Cor. 12:27; Rom. 12:15
wife/husband analogy - Eph. 5:24,25,32

Indwelling Trinity

God the Father
"God abides in us" - I Jn. 4:12,15,16
God the Son
"Christ lives in me" - Gal. 2:20
"Christ in you, the hope of glory" - Col. 1:27
"Jesus Christ is in you" - II Cor. 13:5
God the Spirit
"His Spirit who indwells you" - Rom. 8:11
"Holy Spirit who dwells in us" - II Tim. 1:14

Derived Identity

"sons" because Son lives in us - Gal. 4:6,7
"holy ones" because Holy One lives in us -
Acts 3:14; 4:27,30
"righteous" because Righteous One lives in us-
Acts 3:14; 7:52
"perfect" because Perfect One lives in us -
Heb. 7:28

Christian fully Human

We retain our "personal individuality" and
humanity.
Distinction of "yourself" - Rom. 6:11,13;
II Cor. 13:5; II Tim. 2:15; II Jn. 8; Jude 21

88

BEING
Union

---► **Union**
of Dialectic

━━━━━━━━━━━━━►

Spiritual Union

"The one who is joined to the Lord is one spirit with Him" - I Cor. 6:17

"I have been crucified with Christ, it is no longer I who lives, Christ lives in me" - Gal. 2:20a

Partakers:
"partakers of the divine nature" - II Pet. 1:4
"partakers of Christ" - Heb. 3:1
"partakers of the Holy Spirit" - Heb. 6:4

Fellowship:
"our fellowship with the Father...Son" - I Jn. 1:3
" called into fellowship with Son" - I Cor. 1:9
" fellowship with the Spirit" - Phil. 2:1

"In Christ"
"you are in Christ Jesus"- I Cor 1:30
"Every spiritual blessing in heavenly places in Christ Jesus" - Eph. 1:3
"We are seated in the heavenly places in Christ Jesus" - Eph. 2:6

Life
"Our life is hid with Christ in God" - Col. 3:3
"Christ is our life" - Col. 3:4

Identity Union

"in Christ, a new creature"- II Cor. 5:17
"the new man"- Eph. 4:24; Col. 3:10
"child of God" - Jn. 1:12; Rom. 8:16; I Jn. 3:1,2
"son of God" - Rom. 8:17; Gal. 3:16
"saint" - Rom. 8:27; Eph. 1:18; 4:12
"holy and blameless" - Col. 1:22
"righteous" - Rom. 5:19; II Cor. 5:21
"perfect" - Phil. 3:15; Heb. 10:14; 12:23
"accepted" - Rom. 8:1; 15:7; Eph. 1:6

Collective Identity Union

"people of God" - I Pet. 2:10
"kings and priests" - I Pet. 2:9; Rev. 1:6
"Body of Christ" - Rom. 12:15; I Cor. 12:13

Monistic Merging

Distinction is denied.
Union is lost in "oneness"
"God only" exists *in* and *as* all things.
"God is all in all"
Pantheism, Panentheism
"Only one Person in the universe. (Denial of the Trinity)
"Spirit is the only reality"
Universalism - Christ is intrinsically present in all.

False Union

Essential union of man with God.
- equivalence, absorbed, consubstantial, merged, indistinguishable, fused, coalescence.
Organic Union -
same organism
Hypostatic Union
Christian is deified, divinized, supernaturalized

View of Humanity

Depersonalized reductionism
"I am no longer human."
"I am not; only He is"
Obliteration, annihilation, dissolution, abandonment, displacement, replacement

Union with Christ Diagram #2

⟵――――――

Evangelical Performance

False idea of self-generated
righteous behavior.
"Do your best, God will do
the rest"
"God helps those who help
themselves"
Trying to "be like Jesus.
- imitate Jesus
- follow His example
- Christlikeness

Religion

Christian religion regarded as
- belief-system
- morality and ethics
- role-playing
- problem-solving
Commitment, dedication
Seeking to find "God's will"
Pray more, read Bible more
Increased church involvement
"Serve the Lord"
"Good testimony", witness

Fear, Insecurity, Paranoia

Never know if/when you've
done enough!
Uncertainty, resignation
"I can't help but sin; I'm only
human"
Doubts of salvation

Sin-consciousness

Guilt, shame, condemnation
Suppression, repression
Confessionalism
Hypocrisy

Response-ability

Christians are choosing creatures, responsible
for behavioral choices of faith.
"Apart from Me, you can do nothing" - Jn. 15:5
"I can do all things through Christ" - Phil. 4:13

Faith

Faith is "our receptivity of His activity"
"As received Christ, so walk in Him"- Col. 2:6
"obedience of faith" - Rom. 1:5; 16:26
"faith without works is dead" - James 2:12-26

Imperative Commands

Imperatives are based on indicatives.
Jesus is the *dynamic* of His own *demands.*
"Work out your own salvation" - Phil. 2:12
    "God is at work in you" - Phil. 2:12
"Abstain from every form of evil" - I Th. 5:22
    "He will bring it to pass" - I Thess. 5:24
"Love one another" - Jn. 13:34,35
    "Love of God poured in hearts"- Rom. 5:5
"Discipline self unto godliness" - I Tim. 4:7
    "Everything that is godliness"- II Pt. 1:3
Imperatives of faith
    "Abide in Me" - Jn. 15:5 (settle in, stay put)
    "Reckon yourselves"- Rom. 6:11-*count as fact*
    "Present yourselves" - Rom. 12:1
    "Submit yourselves to God" - James 4:7

Sinful Misrepresentation

"whatever is not of faith, is sin" - Rom. 14:23
"No trial/temptation overtaken you, but is
    common to man" - I Cor. 10:13
"If we say we have no sin, we are deceiving
    ourselves, and truth no in us" - I Jn. 1:8
"Flesh sets its desire against Spirit" - Gal. 5:17
"If we sin, we have Advocate" - I Jn. 2:1

DOING
Union

→ **Union**
of Dialectic

→

Grace Dynamic
Necessary to *behave* like who we have *become*.
"My grace is sufficient for you" - II Cor. 12:9
"God makes all grace abound" - II Cor. 9:8

Trinitarian Action
God the Father
"God is at work in us" - Phil. 2:13
"He will bring it to pass" - I Thess. 5:24
"our adequacy is of God" - II Cor. 3:5
God the Son
"Christ lives in me" - Gal. 2:20
"saved by His life" - Rom. 5:10
"Jesus manifested in us" - II Cor. 4:10,11
God the Spirit
"filled with the Spirit" - Eph. 5:18
"live/walk by the Spirit" - Gal. 5:16,25

Character
"fruit of Spirit - love, joy, peace" - Gal. 5:22,23
"fruit of righteousness" - Eph. 5:9; Phil. 1:11
"bear much fruit" - Jn. 15:5; Col. 1:10
LOVE - "God is love" - I Jn. 4:8,16
"Everyone who loves is born of God" - I Jn. 4:7
Godliness - I Tim. 3:16; II Tim. 3:12; II Pet. 1:3
Holiness - II Tim. 1:9; Heb. 12:10; II Thess. 4:7

Ministry
Spiritual gifts - Rom. 12:6-8; I Cor. 12:1-31
"Ministry of the Spirit" - II cor. 3:6,8
"Ministry of reconciliation" - II Cor. 5:18
"Christ through us" - Acts 15:12; Rom. 15:18,19
"the working of His power" - Eph. 3:7

Collective Union
"unity of the Spirit" - Phil. 1:27; 2:2; Eph. 4:3
"fellowship of sufferings" - Phil. 3:10; Col. 1:24

Determinist Inevitability
Inevitable divine action
Mechanistic oneness that loses
personal relationalism.
"What I do is what He does."
"All I do is Christ in action."

Fatalistic Passivism
Denial of responsibility
Passive instrument of
automatic divine action
Channel or conduit of God
"Just go with the flow"
"God doesn't mean for man to
have faith, but just to be the
God-expressor that he is."

Pride
Gnostic elitism
"Knowers, See-ers, with
superior God-consciousness.
"I do what I will, for what I
will is what He wills."
"Speak the 'word of faith' and
call into being what is not"
"Faith is just speaking your
word."
Co-creators, co-gods

Perfectionism
"Christ can't sin; Christ is the
new man in me. I can't sin."
Sin is an "illusion"
Sin is nothing
Libertine antinomianism
Flaunt alleged liberty.
Disregard for holy behavior

91

CHRIST *IN* US, CHRIST *AS* US, CHRIST *THROUGH* US

Christ *in* us,
Christ *as* us,
Christ *through* us

by

James A. Fowler

Contents

Introduction

The history of Christian theology reveals that there has been far more written about the believer's being "in Christ" than has been written about Christ being present and active *in*, *as*, and *through* the Christian. This is to be expected, in part, because there are far more references in the New Testament to our being "in Christ" than there are to Christ being "in us." But the paucity of emphasis and literature on Christ's internal action in the Christian individual can also be attributed to prevailing emphases within the two major subdivisions of the Western church.

Roman Catholic theology has traditionally taught the infused grace of God in the continuing work of Christ, whereby the empowering energy of God is granted to the Christian in order to live righteously. However, the primary emphasis of Roman theology has been on the collective and corporate realities of Christ's work in the ecclesiastical community of the Roman Church, rather than on the subjective spiritual reality of Christ in individual Christians.

Those in the Church of Rome are regarded to be "in Christ," and there is no salvation apart from the Holy Roman Church. To apply Roman Catholic emphases to the phrases of this study:

Christ is *in* us collectively, for He is in His body, the Church catholic.

Christ is expressed *as* us collectively, for He expresses Himself as the Holy Roman Church.

Christ is expressed *through* us collectively whenever the Catholic Church acts.

This collective and corporate emphasis of the Roman Church has diminished emphasis on the personal and subjective action of Christ in the Christian individual.

In Protestant theology the dearth of emphasis on the subjective presence and activity of Christ in the Christian individual has often not only been the result of an over-collectivized emphasis on Christ's contemporary ecclesiastical action (as in the Roman Catholic Church), but even more so the result of an over-objectified understanding of Christ's work.

Reacting against the Roman emphasis on subjectively infused grade, the Reformers reverted to an almost exclusively objectified reference to redemptive realities that are external and outside of the Christian believer. Protestant theology has traditionally taught the historically objectified acts of Christ in His death, burial, resurrection and ascension *for* us, i.e., on our behalf. In so doing, Christ is also said to have died, risen, and ascended *as* us—as our representative substitute, doing so vicariously in our place.

Christ's historical actions become personally efficacious *for* us when we respond by faith (*sola fide*) and Christ assumes our place *as* us before the heavenly Judge, whereupon the Divine Judge pardons and forgives our sins on the basis of Christ's historically objective actions. In this forensic and juridical framework, God the Judge legally imputes the benefits of Christ's righteousness to us, declares that we are in right standing with Him, and promises a full inheritance of benefits in the future in heaven. All of this action of Christ is outside of—external to—the believer.

D. Martyn Lloyd-Jones wrote: "Justification makes no actual change in us; it is a declaration of God concerning us."[1] Louis Berkhof explained that both Luther and Calvin describe justification "as a forensic act which does not change the inner life of man but only the judicial relationship in which he stands to God."[2] Anglo-Catholic E. L. Mascall notes that "justification has been envisaged as simply an act of God by which man is accounted righteous without any ontological change being made in him."[3] Louis Bouyer, a French Reformed theologian who became Roman Catholic, lamented, "It was apparently impossible for Protestant theology to agree that God could put something in man that became in fact his own, and that at the same time the gift remained the possession of the Giver. That amounts to saying that there can be no real relation between God and man."[4]

These quotations serve to verify that the over-objectification of Protestant theology in general has effectively deterred teaching of the personal and subjective action of Christ in the Christian individual.

A study of the subjective presence and action of the living Lord Jesus *in* us, *as* us, and *through* us is, therefore, outside of the pale of most traditional Western Christian theological teaching, for it runs counter to Protestant over-objectification and Catholic over-collectivization.

It is important to acknowledge, though, that there have been individuals and groups throughout Christian history (some affiliated with both Catholic and Protestant communities, while others were independent of either) that have given due emphasis to the internal presence and action of the living Lord Jesus in the Christian individual. They have often been labeled as "mystics" or "heretics," or both, and many of them paid with their lives for non-conformity to the prevailing and acceptable theological opinions. So, beware—this study may be dangerous to your health!

Prior to considering the subjective presence and action of Christ *in*, *as*, and *through* the Christian individual, it will serve us well to establish some parameters of historic Christian thought that should serve as safeguards against rampant subjectivism that does not remain grounded in biblical tradition. Here are seven proposed tenets of Christian teaching that should not be impinged upon by any consideration of the subjective indwelling and function of Christ in the Christian:

(1) The monotheistic distinction of the Creator God and the creation/creature.
(2) The Trinitarian unity of Being and function in the Godhead.
(3) The anthropological responsibility of man to derive spiritually in freedom of choice.
(4) The harmartiological fall and alienation of man from God in sin.
(5) The historical space and time foundation of the Christian gospel.
(6) The Christological singularity of Christ's Person and work as Savior and Lord.
(7) The soteriological restoration of humanity in regeneration and sanctification.

The institutional church, at large, has been fearful that an emphasis on the subjective relationship of Christ and the Christian would impinge upon the basic foundations of Christian thought. But even more than this concern for ideological preservation has been their concern for ecclesiastical preservation. The tendencies to collectivization and objectification in the Western church have allowed the ecclesiastical authorities to exercise power, maintain control, and "keep a handle on" the Christian enterprise. To allow the grace of God to function freely and subjectively in Christian individuals has been eschewed as a "risky business," allowing for too much individualism, too much subjectivism, and too much personal freedom.

———————— ❧ ————————

The "good news" of the Christian gospel is that
God in Christ is reinvested and restored
in, as, and *through*
the receptive Christian individual.

———————————————————————

The objective of the gospel is not to formulate an orthodox belief-system, nor to construct and maintain an ecclesiastical organization. The Spirit of Christ is free to express the character of Christ in novel and spontaneous ways in each Christian; and that, unto the glory of God. The Holy Spirit must not be imprisoned in church structures, encased in book-interpretations, or relegated only to a judicial courtroom in the heavens.

The Spirit of the living Christ is present *in* the Christian, existing *as* the identity of the Christian, and functioning to express Himself *through* the Christian. The documentation of these realities is the objective of this study.

Chapter 1

Christ *in* us

Despite the attempts of Protestantism to objectify the benefits of Christ's work in an almost paranoid aversion to anything other than "alien righteousness," there have been evangelical Christians throughout the ages who have understood that the Person and work of Jesus Christ must be not only extrinsically applied, but also intrinsically applied; i.e., that the living Person and activity of Christ *indwells* the spirit of the Christian.

This fundamental reality of Christ's actual and spiritual presence within the Christian individual is so well-attested by direct New Testament references that those who "search the scriptures" and are receptive to spiritual reality invariably recognize the indwelling presence of the living Christ.

Jesus Himself explained that He would give another Helper, the Spirit of truth, and His disciples would know that they were in Him, and He was *in* them (John 14:20). In His prayer for unity Jesus explained that He would be *in* His followers as God the Father was *in* Him, the Son (John 17:23).

The apostle Paul clearly noted that the mystery of the gospel is "Christ *in* you, the hope of glory" (Col. 1:27). He asked the Corinthians, "Do you not recognize that Jesus Christ is *in* you?" (II Cor. 13:5), unless you are not a Christian.

_____ ๛ _____

The essential reality that constitutes being a Christian is the indwelling presence of the Spirit of Christ.

_____

"If anyone does not have the Spirit of Christ, he does not belong to Him" (Rom. 8:9), i.e., is not a Christian. Continuing his explanation to the Romans, Paul wrote, "If Christ is *in* you, ...the spirit is alive because of righteousness. If the Spirit of Him Who raised Jesus from the dead dwells *in* you, He Who raised Christ Jesus from the dead will also give life to your mortal bodies through His Spirit Who *indwells* you" (Rom. 8:10,11). The Holy Spirit, the Spirit of Christ, dwells *in* the Christian (cf. John 14:17; Rom. 8:9-11; I Cor. 6:19; II Tim. 1:14; James 4:5), and "bears witness with our spirit that we are children of God" (Rom. 8:16).

The presence of Christ by His Spirit in the Christian is the presence of Himself as spiritual life in the individual. Christ is life. "I am the way, the truth, and the life" (John 14:6), He told His disciples. There can be no spiritual life apart from His presence. Any reference to the Christian having "eternal life" must be understood by the presence of the One Who is life. "He who has the Son has the life; he who does not have the Son of God does not have the life" (I John 5:12). There is no possession of spiritual life apart from the Person Who is life. There is no spiritual benefit apart from the presence of the divine Being of God in Christ. There is no salvation apart from the indwelling presence and activity of the risen and living Savior.

Christian teaching has long referred to "spiritual regeneration," but because of its differing theological biases it has often inadequately indicated what this means.

_____ ☙ _____

To be regenerated is to be "brought into being again" by the reception of divine life in the spirit of an individual.

"That which is born of the Spirit is spirit" (John 3:6). Being "born again" or "born from above" (John 3:3,7) in "new birth" necessarily implies that the personified life of the Spirit of Christ comes to dwell *in* the spirit of an individual who is thus constituted a Christian.

When a person is regenerated, a spiritual exchange takes place.

———————— ❧ ————————

The "spirit that works *in* the sons of disobedience"
(Eph. 2:2), "the spirit of error" (I John 4:6),
"the spirit of this world" (I Cor. 2:12),

is exchanged for

the "Spirit of truth" (I John 4:6),
the "Spirit of God" (I Cor. 2:11,12), the personified
presence of the Spirit of Christ Who works *in* the
Christian (cf. Eph. 3:20; Phil. 2:13; Col. 1:29).

———————————————————

The living Lord Jesus explained to Paul at the time of his conversion that this spiritual exchange was a "turning from darkness to light, and from the dominion of Satan to God" (Acts 26:18).

Regeneration is a spiritual exchange of spiritual personage with*in* the spirit of an individual.

When the New Testament scriptures refer to "Christ *in* us," the Greek preposition used is *en*. The primary meaning of this preposition refers to location or place with*in* something. This locative meaning adequately explains the presence of the Spirit of Christ located *in* the spirit of an individual. A secondary instrumental meaning of the Greek preposition *en* expands the meaning of "Christ *in* us," however. Used in this secondary manner the preposition conveys the meaning of "by means of." Jesus Christ located *in* us is more than a static deposit *in* a particular place *in* the individual. The living Spirit of Christ is always the divine dynamic Who acts and functions "by means of" us. Hence, we begin to see that "Christ *in* us" is foundational to "Christ *as* us" and "Christ *through* us."

When the phrase "Christ *in* us" is used in the instrumental or causal sense of "Christ *by means of* us," it begins to anticipate the other phrases, and to merge or meld into the subsequent phrases of this study. This is why "Christ *in* us" is often employed as a comprehensive phrase to convey Christ's presence and activity in the Christian individual, inclusive of "Christ *as* us" and "Christ *through* us," as it can also include "Christ *by means of* us." The explicit New Testament references to "Christ *in* us" lend credence to its use as an all-inclusive phrase of Christ's presence and function in the Christian.

That Paul meant more by the phrase "Christ *in* you" than just locative placement of the presence of Christ becomes apparent when we examine his statement to the Galatians, "I have been crucified with Christ; and it is no longer I who lives, but Christ *lives in* me" (Gal. 2:20). Christ is *in* us, not merely as a deposit of a commodity called "eternal life," but Christ *lives in* us as the personified and living function of the dynamic of divine life.

If, according to Paul, I am no longer living, and Christ is "*living in* me," then we begin to understand that Christ is living *as* us.

Chapter 2

Christ *as* us

For some readers this will be a phrase they have not previously encountered in popular Christian literature. They may have heard of "Christ *in* us" and "Christ *through* us," but not "Christ *as* us." Admittedly, there is no explicit use of the phrase "Christ *as* us" in the New Testament, and this makes the phrase suspect in the minds of some Christians.

The absence of a direct use of the phrase does not negate its legitimate expression of a biblical and spiritual concept, however. If that were the case, we would have to deny the use of the words "trinity" and "rapture," for these are words not used in scripture, but they most certainly express biblical concepts and are commonly employed in Christian terminology. In like manner, "Christ *as* us" is a phrase that conveys an important biblical theme not fully encompassed in the other phrases.

As noted above, "Christ *in* us" refers in its primary meaning to the location and placement of the presence of Christ within the spirit of a receptive individual. In its secondary meaning it refers to "Christ *by means of* us," but still does not carry with it the connotation of what the believer has become because of the presence and function of Jesus Christ within.

Are we merely an occupied spirit-space? Or an invaded spirit-being? Or are we something or someone that we were not, before we became a Christian? Does the spiritual exchange create a change in us? When we are regeneratively "brought into being again," do we become different than we were previously? Or do we just receive an "eternal life" package by the placement of the Spirit of Christ within the location of our spirit?

_____ ☙ _____

The biblical evidence reveals that the Christian becomes something or someone that he/she was not, prior to becoming a Christian.

_____

Paul explains, "If anyone is in Christ, he is a new creature; the old things have passed away; behold all things have become new" (II Cor. 5:17). The unregenerate "old man" (Eph. 4:22; Col. 3:9), worthy of death by personal accountability for sin, "has been crucified with Christ" (Rom. 6:6).

A New Identity

By spiritual regeneration a Christian becomes a "new man" (Eph. 4:24; Col. 3:10) in Christ. Christians are transformed from being "a natural man" (I Cor. 2:14) into being "spiritual men" (I Cor. 3:1). Whereas they once were "children of the devil" (I John 3:10) and "sons of disobedience" (Eph. 2:2; 5:6), they are now "children of God" (John 1:12; Rom. 8:16; I John 3:1,2,10) and "sons of God" (Rom. 8:14,17; II Cor. 6:18; Gal. 3:26; 4:6,7; Heb. 2:10).

By the presence and function of Jesus Christ within their spirit, believers are identified as "Christians" (Acts 11:26; I Pet. 4:16), indicating that they are Christ-ones. All of these biblical expressions and designations evidence the new *identity* of the one in whom Christ dwells and lives.

Regeneration, the indwelling presence of the living Lord Jesus, does have the effect of making a person something that he was not before, a "new creature" with a new identity. Who we are as Christians is based on Who Christ is *in* us and *as* us, constituting us as Christ-ones. "Christ *as* us" is, therefore, a phrase that expresses our new identity in a way that the other phrases cannot convey.

Some might object that the "Christ *as* us" phrase, dealing as it does with identity, is just addressing a psychological need of modern man to have an individualized sense of self-identity, self-image, self-awareness, self-consciousness, self-concept, self-worth, etc. Not so! The phrase is not used to explain a psychological need or phenomenon, but to explain a spiritual reality of the Christian life. There are scriptural statements in abundance relating to the fact that the Christian has become something and someone that he/she was not previously.

_____ ☙ _____

At the very core of the Christian's being,
in the innermost function of the human spirit,
the Christian has become a new person
with a new identity.

Psychology deals with the distinctive of our individuality in differing personalities, often referred to as a "perceived sense of identity in the psyche," but the deepest level of identity is always in the spirit of a person; and that, in derived association and union with the spiritual being that indwells that person's spirit.

"Christ *as* us" refers to our identity as Christians by reason of His real spiritual presence and His being Who He is in us.

"Christ is our life" (Col. 3:4), and Christians "live together with" (I Thess. 5:10) and "through" (I John 4:9) Him. "Christ has become to us righteousness" (I Cor. 1:30). "We become the righteousness of God in Him" (II Cor. 5:21) when we

16

are "created in righteousness" (Eph. 4:24) as a "new man" and are "made righteous" (Rom. 5:19). As "new creatures in Christ" (II Cor. 5:17), Christians are "created in holiness" (Eph. 4:24) and are "holy and beloved" (Col. 3:12) as "holy ones" or "saints" (cf. Rom. 1:7; 8:27; Eph. 1:18; 4:12). In Christ we are "perfect" (Phil. 3:15) and "sanctified" (Heb. 10:14) as "righteous men made perfect" (Heb. 12:23), for Christ "has become to us wisdom and sanctification" (I Cor. 1:24,30).

Jesus Christ becomes the basis of the spiritual identity of the Christian, but we must always understand that this is a derived identity, a derived life, a derived righteousness, holiness and perfection.

These are not realities that we have become essentially or inherently in and by ourselves, but only by His presence within us. We are made righteous only because Christ, the "Righteous One" (Acts 3:14; 7:52; 22:14; I John 2:1), dwells and functions *in* us and *as* us. Christians are said to be "holy" and "perfect" only because Jesus Christ is the "Holy One" (Acts 3:14; 4:27,30), the One "made perfect forever" (Heb. 7:28), Who has become the basis of our derived identity.

"Christ *as* us" is another way of referring to the Christian's "union with Christ" which has been a part of Christian understanding from the beginning of the church. Christian thinkers have often struggled, however, to explain and articulate what Paul meant by his statement, "The one being joined to the Lord is one spirit (with Him)" (I Cor. 6:17).

17

Likewise, they have shied away from Peter's assertion that Christians "have become partakers of the divine nature" (II Peter 1:4). Clinging to the Greek humanistic idea of an inherent "human nature," Christians have often been blinded to the scriptural explanation that "we were by nature (Greek *phusis*) children of wrath" (Eph. 2:3) in our unregenerate spiritual condition, when "the prince of the power of the air, the spirit that works in the sons of disobedience" (Eph. 2:2), was indwelling and operative in us, but we are now "partakers of the divine nature *(phusis)*" (II Pet. 1:4), by the presence and function of "the Spirit of Christ" (Rom. 8:9) within the spirit of the Christian (cf. Rom. 8:16).

Being "partakers (*koinonoi*) of the divine nature" (II Pet. 1:4) and "partakers (*metachoi*) of Christ" (Heb. 3:14) implies that Christians are participants in Christ, sharing in the commonality of His nature and identity in spiritual union with Him. This participatory fellowship (*koinonia*) with the living Lord Jesus (I Cor. 1:9), with God the Father (I John 1:3,6), and with the Holy Spirit (Phil. 2:1) indicates a spiritual union with the Triune Godhead.

This discussion of the Christian's spiritual identity in "union with Christ" raises a question: Is it legitimate to allow the phrase "Christ *as* us" to mean "Christ *is* us"? We have previously noted that Paul wrote, "Christ *is* our life" (Col. 3:4) and "Christ has become to us righteousness" (I Cor. 1:30; II Cor. 5:21). Our explanation has been that Christ *is* the basis of our new identity as a "new creature" (II Cor. 5:17), a "new man" (Eph. 4:24; Col. 3:10) in Him.

Christ *is* the essence of who we are as Christ-ones, as Christians; the essence of our spiritual identity. Does this allow, then, for a legitimate usage of the phrase, "Christ *is* us"? Our logical syllogisms, grammatical phrases, and spiritual understanding must be carefully stated at this point. Though we might say "Christ *is* us" in a qualified manner, is this to be interpreted in such a way that the equation can be turned around and stated, "We are Christ" or "I am Christ"?

Without qualification such statements would be blasphemous! To claim to *be* God the Father, God the Son, or God the Holy Spirit is to claim the essence of deity. This violates the monotheistic premise that Who (and what) God *is*, only God *is*.

To claim to *be* Christ impinges upon several of the seven foundational tenets of Christian teaching that we noted in the introduction to this study, particularly the monotheistic distinction of the Creator and the creature, the Trinitarian unity of the Godhead, and the Christological singularity of Christ's Person and work.

References to "Christ *as* us" and "Christ *is* us," and statements like "I am Jesus Christ in John Doe form," must be carefully explained so that any implication of the Christian's being equivalent to Christ is avoided. These phrases push the limits of the fine-line of demarcation that allows for a valid

19

expression of the Christian's "union with Christ" wherein Christ is expressed *as* us, and the recognition, on the other hand, that the human individual is always a receptive, contingent and derivative creature distinguished from the essence of the Creator, God.

Previous mention was made of the two major branches of the Western church, both Roman Catholic and Protestant, and how they have avoided reference to the subjective indwelling of Christ in the Christian individual by the over-collectivization of ecclesiasticism and the over-objectification of a law-based theology.

There is another major segment of the Christian church at large that has been long neglected by Western Christianity. The Eastern Orthodox Church —which includes the Greek, Russian, Cyprian and Serbian national churches—has a sustained history from the commencement of Christianity. This branch of the church has traditionally cited the statements of the early church fathers concerning the Christian's participation in the divine nature in ways that make the Western church very uncomfortable. Here are some examples of such statements:

> "Our Lord Jesus Christ...became what we are, so that He might bring us to be even what He Himself is." – Irenaeus, c. A.D. 180[5]

> "The man of God is consequently divine and is already holy. He is God-bearing and God-borne." – Clement of Alexandria, c. A.D. 195[6]

"You will be a companion of God, and a co-heir with Christ... For you have become divine... God has promised to bestow these upon you, for you have been deified and begotten unto immortality." – Hippolytus, c. A.D. 225[7]

"...from Him there began the union of the divine with the human nature. This was so that the human – by communion with the divine – might rise to be divine. This not only happened in Jesus, but also in all those who not only believe, but enter upon the life that Jesus taught." – Origen, c. A.D. 248[8]

"What man is, Christ was willing to be – so that man may also be what Christ is." – Cyprian, c. A.D. 250[9]

"God became man so that man might become God." – Athanasius, c. A.D. 325[10]

"God has called men 'gods' that are deified of His Grace, not born of His Substance." – Augustine, c. A.D. 400[11]

The Eastern church refers to this participation of the Christian in the divine nature as *Theosis* or "deification." This is strange-sounding terminology to most Western Christians. Eastern Orthodox theologians are careful to explain, though, that neither the early church fathers nor they are advocating that the Christian becomes God. They qualify "deification" by indicating that it is participation in the "energies" of God's presence and Being, rather than becoming the "essence" of the

Being of God. Though they emphasize the intimacy of the union of the Christian with the "divine nature," they maintain at the same time that the creature always remains essentially distinct from God. They maintain a careful balance of union and distinction.

Protestant evangelicals in the Western church are reluctantly admitting that the Eastern Orthodox teaching of *Theosis* or "deification" does not impinge upon the foundational teachings of Christianity, such as the seven basic tenets enumerated in the introduction of this study. Robert M. Bowman, Jr., writing in the *Christian Research Journal*, states:

> It may surprise some to learn that a monotheistic doctrine of deification was taught by many of the church fathers, and is believed by many Christians today, including the entire Eastern Orthodox Church. In keeping with monotheism, the Eastern orthodox do not teach that men will literally become 'gods' (which would be polytheism). Rather, as did many of the church fathers, they teach that men are 'deified' in the sense that the Holy Spirit dwells within Christian believers and transforms them into the image of God in Christ... Thus, it should not be argued that anyone who speaks of deification necessarily holds to a heretical view of man. Such a sweeping judgment would condemn many of the early church's greatest theologians (e.g., Athanasius, Augustine), as well as one of the three main branches of historic orthodox Christianity in existence today.[12]

Alan F. Johnson and Robert Webber, theology professors at Wheaton College, write in their book, *What Christians Believe*:

The first clearly articulated concept of the application of the work of Christ to the sinful human condition is developed in the East... This view is known as *theosis* or deification. ...This does not mean, as it may appear on the surface, that humanity shares in the essence of God. Human persons do not become God. Rather, because the work of Christ destroys the powers of evil, we are freed from those powers and able to come into fellowship with God... His redeemed creatures have been given the benefits and privileges of divinity through grace. The state of grace is seen as a state of communion with God, fellowship with the Trinity, a partaking of the divine.[13]

F. W. Norris, professor at Emmanuel School of Religion, wrote an article entitled "Deification: Consensual and Cogent" in the *Scottish Journal of Theology*, indicating:

...patristic theologians offered a remarkable view of what Protestants refer to as "restoration" or "fellowship." These theologians ground it in a sense of Christian salvation: *theosis* or deification. ...No universal Christian consensus demands that one view of salvation includes or excludes all others.[14]

Poorly-read Protestants have insisted that the Eastern Orthodox idolatrously make us all little gods or that they think of participation in the divine nature only in physical terms. These charges are false. Orthodox theologians keep deification away from Gnostic or Manichaean speculation, or what we might recognize as the worst aspects of Far Eastern mysticism and now so-called New Age musings.[15]

We Christians have the promise of participating in the divine nature. ...Not only Eastern Orthodox but also Western theologians find solace in a sense of deification. Such restoration does not mean that we become God as the Father, Son and Holy Spirit are God. Our participation in the divine nature is in God's energies, not the essence, a participation through grace accepted in faith which includes being participants in Christ's sufferings.[16]

More than any other in the context of recent Protestant evangelicalism, the British missionary statesman and author Norman P. Grubb emphasized the truth of "Christ *as* us." It was the distinctive of his ministry to compel Christians to recognize their spiritual identity in Christ. The titles of his later books reveal this emphasis: *Who Am I?*[17] and *Yes I Am.*[18]

Grubb was very careful, however, to emphasize that the Christian's spiritual union with Christ did not mean "a relationship of total absorption."[19] "The idea that we can be deified – that is blasphemy,"[20] Grubb wrote. "The essence of idolatry is to claim to be what only God is..."[21] "The creature never becomes the Creator."[22] "The container never becomes the contents." "We are the creature, He the Creator, neither one becoming the other."[23] "Our oneness with Christ does not alter our two-ness."[24] "The human spirit...can be the container of the Divine Spirit...and yet not lose its own individuality in so being."[25] "The human is forever the human, and the divine the divine."[26] In these, and many other ways, Norman

Grubb attempted to balance the union and distinction, unity and diversity, oneness and two-ness of the relationship of Christ and the Christian.

Having considered some biblical bases for "union with Christ" and some theological background of how others have explained participation in the divine nature, it will now be beneficial to return to the consideration of the phrase "Christ *as* us" in order to do a brief grammatical study of the English word "as."

In the English language the word "as" can be employed as an adverb, a conjunction, a preposition, and even as a pronoun.

- Adverbially, "as" means "equivalent to" or "the same as." Used adverbially, "Christ *as* us" would mean "Christ is the *same as* us" or "Christ *is as* we are (I am)."

- Used as a conjunction, "as" means "in the same manner" or "to the same degree." The "Christ *as* us" phrase would then mean "Christ, in *like manner as* us."

- Our utilization of the "Christ *as* us" phrase in this study is primarily considering the word in the prepositional usage, where "as" refers to "function, role or capacity."
    "Christ serves *as* the identity of us."
    "Christ functions *as* us."
    "Christ expresses Himself *as* us."

In like manner as the "Christ *in* us" and "Christ *through* us" phrases are prepositional, we are using "Christ *as* us" as a prepositional phrase also.

"Christ *as* us" means more than "Christ *as if He were* us" in an unreal and hypothetical fashion. The "Christ *as* us" phrase also means more than "Christ, *as it were*, so to speak, us" in a merely figurative and illustrative analogy. If the "Christ *as* us" phrase is interpreted as "Christ, *represented as* us," we must beware of any implications that Christ is just a sign or symbol represented in our lives, or that the Christian is "playing the part" or "taking the place of" Christ. On the other hand, there is legitimacy in the interpretation that "Christ is *re-presented as* us" in a contemporary manifestation of His life.

The meaning of the phrase "Christ *as* us," as used in this study, can be reduced to two primary prepositional emphases: (1) Christ functioning *as* us in terms of the identity of our being. (2) Christ functioning *as* us in terms of the instrumentality of our activity. In other words, (1) Christ expressed ontologically *as* us. (2) Christ expressed operationally *as* us. The first of these has to do with the Being of Christ serving as the basis of the Christian's being and identity. The second of these has to do with the activity of Christ serving as the basis of the Christian's expression and behavior.

These two aspects of "union with Christ," ontological union and operational union, are integrally united in the unity of God's Being and action. God's Being is always expressed in His action, and His action is always invested with and expressive of His Being. In other words, there can be no detachment or separation in Who God *is* and what God *does*. In like manner, our behavior as Christians should be expressive of who we have become in Christ.

Behavioral Manifestation

Our study of "Christ *as* us" has (to this point) focused primarily on the ontological sense of identity, so we now turn our attention to the operational sense of Christ's functioning *as* us in behavioral manifestation. Christ operating *as* us in the expression of Himself will eventually begin to merge into the meaning of "Christ *through* us," but in order to differentiate the emphases we will reserve the "Christ *through* us" phrase for the expression of Christ that extends beyond us to others.

"Christ manifested *as* us" implies the living reality of the presence of Christ *in* us, the basis of our new spiritual identity in our union with Christ *as* us. Christ cannot remain dormant within us as a static deposit of identification. The living Lord Jesus must of necessity express Himself dynamically as Who He is in our behavior.

The Christian life is not a self-generated expression of moral and ethical behavior that attempts to conform to the example of Christ, and thereby be Christ-like. Rather, the Christian life is the

Christ-life, Christ "living in me" (Gal. 2:20), lived out *as* me.

Despite the misconceptions that abound in the religious thinking of many Christians today, the objective of the Christian life is not an imitation of the life of Jesus, but the manifestation of the very life of Jesus. Paul wrote to the Corinthians, "We have this treasure (Christ) in earthen vessels (human bodies), that the surpassing greatness of the power may be of God and not from ourselves; ...that the life of Jesus may be *manifested* in our body, ...*manifested* in our mortal flesh" (II Cor. 4:7,10,11).

------------------ ঔ ------------------

The Christian life is not imitation, but *manifestation* of Jesus *as* us!

When Christ is expressed *as* us, manifesting His life and character in our behavior, this creates a unique re-presentation (see above) of Christ's life. Christians are not meant to be carbon copy, cookie-cutter conformists operating in Xerox uniformity.

Utilizing our unique individualities and personalities, Christ lives out His life *as* us. This is accomplished in the spontaneity of allowing Jesus to function and express His character in whatever role or capacity we find ourselves, whether as husband or wife, employer or employee, leader or follower, etc.

By faith the Christian allows for the receptivity of His active character expressed *as* us.

Ever since the writings of the early church fathers, many have referred to the active expression of "Christ *as* us" as the incarnational reality of Christianity. The historical incarnation of Jesus has often been made analogous to the relationship of Christ and the Christian. It has been noted that:

God was *in* the man, Jesus
(Matt. 1:23; John 17:21),
was incarnated *as* the man, Jesus
(John 1:14; Phil. 2:7-11), and
was acting *through* the man, Jesus
(John 14:10; Acts 2:22).

The Christological incarnation of the Son of God is not identical, however, to the expression of "Christ *as* us." The incarnation of the Word of God involved the hypostatic union of God and man unified in one person, who was the singular mediator between God and man (I Tim. 2:5) as the God-man.

Whenever the idea of incarnation is applied to Christians it must be in a generalized sense of the life and activity of the living Lord Jesus embodied "*in* us" and enfleshed "*as* us" as we functionally express Christ's life. This does not invalidate references to the contemporary incarnational expression of "Christ *as* us," but does reveal the necessity of always recognizing the difference between Christ's incarnation and the incarnational expression of Christ's life in our behavior.

The process of allowing for the expression of Christ's life in our behavior is called "sanctification." To be sanctified is not to achieve a sanctimonious piety by particular religious disciplines or by peculiar conformity of dress and behavior. To be sanctified is, rather, to allow Jesus, the Holy One (Acts 3:14; 4:27,30), Who lives *in* us *as* the basis of our new spiritual identity, to express His holy character in the actions of our behavior. Thus, we are set apart to function as God intended, expressing His holy character "in spirit and soul and body" (I Thess. 5:23).

A verse often cited to document "Christ's function *as* us" is found in John's first epistle. In the context of referring to God's love being perfected, i.e., brought to its intended end in expression towards others, John writes, "As He is, so are we in this world" (I John 4:17). The contextual meaning seems to be that "just as (*kathos*) Christ is the functional expression of God's love to others (mankind - cf. John 3:16), so also we (Christians) are the functionally expressive agents of God's love within the world of mankind where we live."

John's underlying assumption is that "Christ *as* us" (identity) will express God's divine love "*as* us" (activity) in consistent expression of the character of God (which is the primary thrust of John's epistle). This verse does refer to "Christ's function *as* us" in expressing God's love, but should not be wrenched from its context to mean "as Christ is in His essential Being, so we are in our essential being."

Christ functions as us by actually and actively living His life in us (Gal. 2:20).

Christians are "saved by His life" (Rom. 5:10), and set free to function as God intended and as God energizes. Controlled and "filled with His Spirit" (Eph. 5:18), Christians manifest the "fruit of the Spirit" (Gal. 5:22,23), "the fruit of righteousness" (Eph. 5:9; Phil. 1:11; Heb. 12:11), which is the character of Christ.

Again, this is not a character that Christians generate or actuate from their own energies and "works," but Christian character is only and always derived from Christ. Christians allow for the outworking of Christ's activity to which they are receptive in faith (James 2:17-26), engaging in "good works which were prepared beforehand that they should walk in them" (Eph. 2:10), as God "works in them that which is pleasing in His sight" (Heb. 13:21).

Only by "Christ's function *as* us" do we "live godly in Christ Jesus" (II Tim. 3:12), to the glory of God (I Cor. 10:31; II Cor. 3:18; I Pet. 4:11), which is the purpose for which we were created (cf. Isa. 43:7).

Chapter 3

Christ *through* us

Jesus Christ functionally expressing His life *as* us necessarily merges into an understanding of "Christ *through* us." As previously explained, the operational union of Christ *as* us, expressing His life and character through our behavior, was addressed in the previous section; whereas Christ functioning *through* us in extension to other persons will be the focus of our explanation here. These concepts are obviously integrated and should not be made into rigid categories or definitions. Much of our explanation of Christ's operational function *as* us could just as well have been explained as Christ's functional expression *through* us.

Having noted how the character of Christ is expressed in Christian behavior by "the fruit of the Spirit" (Gal. 5:22,23), we now note that **the ministry of Christ is performed *through* us by the "gifts of the Spirit"** (cf. Rom. 12; I Cor. 12; Eph. 4:8-16). The "fruit of the Spirit" has to do with the functional expression of the character of Christ, while the "gifts of the Spirit" have to do with the ministry of Christ to others in the context of the body of Christ (the church).

It is most lamentable that in many portions of the church today, the "gifts of the Spirit" are regarded as marks of spirituality or trophies of spiritual possession, rather than as the means of Christ's ministry *through* Christians. The "gifts of the Spirit" should not be viewed as separated or detached entities or abilities, but only as the functional grace-expressions by which Christ ministers *through* any Christian in a given situation of another's need. (cf. Fowler, *Charismata: the so-called "Spiritual Gifts"*)

The ministry activity of Jesus Christ during His historical, earthly ministry was accomplished as "the man Christ Jesus" (I Tim. 2:5) was the "man attested by God with miracles and wonders and signs which God performed *through* Him" (Acts 2:22). Jesus carefully explained that He did nothing of His own initiative (John 5:19,30; 8:28; 12:49; 14:10), but declared, "the Father abiding in Me does His works" (John 14:10).

―――――――― ❧ ――――――――

How did Jesus do what He did
in His earthly ministry?
Even the "miracles and wonders and signs" were
what "God performed *through* Him."

Doctor Luke later wrote that "the multitude were listening to Barnabas and Paul as they were relating what signs and wonders God had done *through* them among the Gentiles" (Acts 15:12). In like manner as Jesus ministered by being receptive to God's activity *through* Him, the apostles ministered in supernatural ways as God functioned *through* them.

Writing to the Romans, Paul explained, "I do not presume to speak of anything except what Christ has accomplished *through* me, resulting in the obedience of the Gentiles by word and deed, in the power of signs and wonders, in the power of the Spirit" (Rom. 15:18,19). This is obviously a very explicit reference to Christ's function *through* the Christian.

The Greek word used in these references just cited is the Greek preposition *dia,* which has a primary and direct meaning of procession *through* an object, place, or person. It often conveys the meaning of extension *through* that goes beyond and out from the object, place, or person. This idea of extension beyond ourselves unto others is important in the understanding of "Christ *through* us" as Christians.

A secondary, instrumental meaning of *dia* is "by means of," which allows the word to have the same secondary meaning as the Greek preposition *en,* revealing that these prepositions tend to overlap one another in meaning and must not be treated with rigid precision.

The presence and function of the living Jesus *in*, *as*, and *through* the Christian is not for the purpose or objective of making us spiritually bloated "knowers," full of pride in our alleged "spirituality" and what we "know" as Gnostic elitists. The only thing, the only One, we know is Him, Jesus Christ, in an ontological knowing of relational intimacy, rather than an epistemological knowledge of data that merely puffs us up in arrogance (I Cor. 8:1).

The One we know is Jesus. Jesus is God (John 10:30). God is love (I John 4:8,16). God as love is a Self Who has no needs and exists only for others, expressing Himself in grace and love and givingness. Therefore, when Jesus functions *in* us, and *as* us, and *through* us, He is always expressing Himself in grace and love for others.

In the epistle to the Hebrews it is written, "Christ always lives to make intercession..." (Heb. 7:25), for His is a permanent priesthood (Heb. 7:24). In that case, He must live *in* us, and *as* us, and *through* us to make intercession for others. Christians have long advocated "intercessory prayer" for others, but seldom have they considered what it means to engage in "intercessory lives" or "intercessory ministry" for others.

The intent of God in Christ was to provide for "a kingdom of priests" (Exod. 19:6) who would function as a royal intercessory priesthood (I Peter 2:9) as "priests of the Lord and ministers of God" (Isa. 61:6) for others. Christians are that kingdom of priests (Rev. 1:6; 5:10), wherein the sacrificial and intercessory character of God is to function for others.

_____ ❧ _____

Without thought for Himself, Jesus "laid down His life" (John 10:17,18; I John 3:16) for others, and as He lives *in* and *through* the Christian He will continue to express the same self-sacrifice, self-surrender, and self-giving that is inherent in God's character.

_____

As Christians "lay down their lives for the brethren" (I John 3:16), it is not for the same redemptive and propitiatory purpose which was singularly fulfilled by the Person of Christ, but the same willingness to be an expendable investiture for others remains.

Christians thereby begin to recognize that participation and fellowship (*koinonia*) with Christ is not only the commonality of union with Him in an identity that expresses itself *as* us, but also involves participating in "the fellowship (*koinonia*) of His sufferings" (Phil. 3:10).

As Paul invested himself in ministry unto others, he indicated that he was "filling up what was lacking in Christ's affliction" (Col. 1:24) because Christ continued to suffer *in* and *as* him. "The sufferings of Christ are ours in abundance" (II Cor. 1:5), but "we suffer with Him that we might be glorified with Him" (Rom. 8:17), Paul wrote in other letters. "Christ through us" involves being willing "to stand in the gap" (Ezek. 22:30) for others, recognizing that our present physical bodies and lives are expendable since we have the spiritual continuity and perpetuity of Christ's eternal life.

"Christ *through* us" is the extension of Christ's ministry *through* Christians. The objective of that ministry is not for self-indulgent progression unto knowledge or spirituality, but is always Christ giving Himself to and for others *in* us, *as* us, and *through* us.

Conclusion

The phrases we have considered in this study—
"Christ *in* us," "Christ *as* us," and "Christ *through*
us"—are not necessarily to be understood as
progressive, successive or sequential steps or stages
of spiritual knowledge or spiritual growth. Though
we have differentiated between them, they often meld
and merge into an integrated and comprehensive
emphasis of "Christ *by means of* us," as this is a
permissible interpretation of all three prepositions.

We should avoid analyzing the meaning of these
three phrases too precisely or rigidly, allowing the
living reality of Christ to express Himself as He will.

It is questionable whether the realities to which
these phrases refer should be cast into separate
theological categories as some have done, attempting
to represent them as justification, sanctification, and
glorification; or as regeneration, unification, and
ministration. Even illustrative analogies such as
John's reference to "children, young men, and
fathers" (I John 2:12-14) are best avoided, as these
are often misleading.

When an individual is regenerated by the receipt of the Spirit of Christ into his/her spirit (Rom. 8:9), Christ is *in* that person, immanently indwelling them; Christ forms their identity, functioning *as* them, for Christ cannot help but act as the Being that He is; and Christ is living *through* them, laying down His life in intercessory ministry for others.

Despite the caution of defining these internal spiritual realities too precisely, the following differentiations may be helpful for general definition.

"Christ *in* us" has to do with indwelling.
"Christ *as* us" has to do with identity.
"Christ *through* us" has to do with intercession.

The preposition "in" refers to location; the preposition "as" refers to function; the preposition "through" refers to extension. "Christ *in* us" points to *Presence*—the real *presence* of the living Lord Jesus *in* our spirit; "Christ *as* us" suggests *Identity*—His presence establishes our new *identity as* Christ-ones; "Christ *through* us" implies *Expression*—Christ's presence and function necessitates His *expression through* us unto others.

In conclusion let us note that Paul wrote of the Corinthians "being manifested as a letter of Christ, ...written not with ink, but with the Spirit of the living God...on tablets of human hearts" (II Cor. 3:3). Christ living *by means of* us creates a unique living epistle that *re-presents* Christ to others in the contemporary form of our own lives. Such a presentation of Christ *in* us, and *as* us, and *through* us, may be the only living form of Jesus that another person may ever observe.

This adaptation of another's verse seems to capture the point poetically:

Christ is writing a letter *in* you each day.
The message, that is Him, must be true.
'Tis the only Jesus that some men will see –
The life of Christ expressed *as* and *through* YOU.

_____ ❧ _____

Endnotes

1 Lloyd-Jones, D. Martyn, *Romans: Atonement and Justification: An Exposition of Chapters 3:20–4:25.* Grand Rapids: Zondervan Pub. House. 1970. pg. 55.
2 Berkhof, Louis, *The History of Christian Doctrines.* Grand Rapids: Baker Book House. 1975. pg. 220.
3 Mascall, E. L., *Christ, the Christian and the Church: A Study of the Incarnation and its Consequences.* London: Longmans. 1959. pg. 81.
4 Bouyer, Louis, *The Spirit and Forms of Protestantism.* London: The Harvill Press. 1956. pg. 151.
5 Irenaeus, *Against Heresies.* Book V, Preface. Series: The Ante-Nicene Fathers, Vol. I. Grand Rapids: Wm. B. Eerdmans Pub. Co., 1985 ed., pg. 526.
6 Clement of Alexandria, *The Stromata.* Book VII, Chapter XIII. Series: The Ante-Nicene Fathers, Vol. II. Grand Rapids: Wm. B. Eerdmans Pub. Co., 1985 ed., pg. 547.
7 Hippolytus, *The Refutation of All Heresies.* Book X, Chapter XXX. Series: The Ante-Nicene Fathers, Vol. V. Grand Rapids: Wm. B. Eerdmans Pub. Co., 1985 ed., pg. 153.

8 Origen, *Against Celsus*. Book III, Chapter XXVIII. Series: The Ante-Nicene Fathers, Vol. IV. Grand Rapids: Wm. B. Eerdmans Pub. Co., 1985 ed., pg. 475.

9 Cyprian, *Treatise VI, On the Vanity of Idols*. Series: The Ante-Nicene Fathers, Vol. V. Grand Rapids: Wm. B. Eerdmans Pub. Co., 1985 ed., pg. 468.

10 Athanasius, *On the Incarnation of the Word*. Part III, No. 54. Series: A Select Library of the Nicene and Post-Nicene Fathers of the Christian Church. Second Series, Vol. IV. 1983 ed., pg. 65.

11 Augustine, *Exposition of the Psalms*. Psalm 50:2. Series: A Select Library of the Nicene and Post-Nicene Fathers of the Christian Church. First Series, Vol. VIII. 1983 ed., pg. 178.

12 Bowman, Robert M., Jr., "Ye are Gods? Orthodox and Heretical Views on the Deification of Man." Article in *Christian Research Journal*. Winter/Spring 1987. pg. 18.

13 Johnson, Alan F. and Webber, Robert, *What Christians Believe: A Biblical and Historical Summary*. Grand Rapids: Zondervan Pub. House. 1993. pg. 303.

14 Norris, F. W., "Deification: Consensual and Cogent." Article in *Scottish Journal of Theology*. Vol. 49, No. 4. 1996. pg. 412.

15 *Ibid.*, pg. 418.

16 *Ibid.*, pg. 428.

17 Grubb, Norman P., *Who Am I?* Fort Washington: Christian Literature Crusade. 1974.

18 Grubb, Norman P., *Yes I Am*. Fort Washington: Christian Literature Crusade. 1982.

19 Grubb, Norman P., *God Unlimited*. Fort Washington: Christian Literature Crusade. 1989. pg. 158.

20 Grubb, Norman P., *The Key to Everything* (booklet). Fort Washington: Christian Literature Crusade. 1960. pg. 23.

21 Grubb, Norman P., *The Deep Things of God*. Fort Washington: Christian Literature Crusade. 1974. pg. 9.

22 Grubb, *Who Am I? op. cit.*, pg. 95.

23 Grubb, Norman P., *The Spontaneous You*. Fort Washington: Christian Literature Crusade. 1972. pg. 54.

24 Grubb, *Yes I Am. op. cit.*, pg. 132.

25 Grubb, Norman P., *The Liberating Secret*. Fort Washington: Christian Literature Crusade. 1978. pg. 39.

26 Grubb, *The Key to Everything. op. cit.*, pg. 24.